Date Due

DEC 15 '77			
MAY 0 3 1990			

BRODART PRINTED IN U.S.A.

TWENTIETH CENTURY VIEWS

The aim of this series is to present the best in contemporary critical opinion on major authors, providing a twentieth century perspective on their changing status in an era of profound revaluation.

Maynard Mack, *Series Editor*
Yale University

KEATS

KEATS

A COLLECTION OF CRITICAL ESSAYS

Edited by

Walter Jackson Bate

Prentice-Hall, Inc. *Englewood Cliffs, New Jersey*

Current printing (last digit):

13

 Library of Congress Catalog Card Number 64-23562. Printed in the United States of America (C). P51474, C51475

Table of Contents

KEATS

Introduction

by Walter Jackson Bate

I

No English poet since the middle of the seventeenth century seems to have attracted a wider variety of readers, and for a more nearly unbroken period of time, than Keats. Almost every other poet has suffered periods either of comparative neglect or of a drop in critical esteem (the two do not necessarily go together). Dryden and Pope were under a general cloud of disapproval from the early 1800s until the 1920s, and Blake acquired a secure position as a major poet only during the generation after World War I. Byron's reputation, which began to sink in the mid-nineteenth century, is only now beginning to recover. Others of the romantics (even Wordsworth to some extent, certainly Shelley), as well as most of the Victorians, were roughly treated in the wholesale revolt against the nineteenth century that became so militant in the 1920s and '30s. But the interest in Keats, already strong by the 1850s, has become more deeply rooted with every decade. In the period between the two World Wars, even the most single-minded opponents of all that the nineteenth century was said to represent (romantic emotionalism, the cult of revery, naturalism, representational art) dropped their weapons when they came to Keats and found themselves regarding him not only with admiration but a rather strong personal sympathy. Several explanations are possible. Three in particular stand out, in ascending importance, and appear to subsume most of the others.

First, there is the personal interest of Keats's life, so vividly compressed in the short period of twenty-five years. To begin with, the story of his life has something of the perennial appeal of folklore—the orphan cast adrift and compelled to seek his own fortune. There is a villain in this Dickensian tale—the unscrupulous tea-merchant, Richard Abbey, who served as guardian to the Keats children and appropriated money that was due them; there is Keats's moving love-affair with Fanny Brawne;

episodes of courage and generosity continue to occur, almost month by month; we encounter a gallery of fairly colorful minor characters; and finally, after the onset of his fatal illness, there are the terrible last months, the long journey to Italy, and Keats's death in Rome. For these reasons alone, any number of people during the last century not generally much concerned with poetry have still been interested in Keats's life. (Much the same thing has happened with Samuel Johnson.) Every scrap of information has been collected, discussed, rediscussed, and often used as a basis for speculation that may have little to do with any important aspect of Keats's work but at least tends to show how closely (if subjectively) radically different people can become identified with Keats.

Second, and of deeper (and ultimately wider) interest, is the drama of Keats's achievement—his astonishing development as a mind and a writer in the course of only four or five years. Indeed, without this, the more external events of Keats's life, however readable in themselves, would lack the almost allegorical value that continues to sustain our interest. He is one of those rare figures who, through what they did and became, induce our thinking to return to basic questions and premises. All of us wonder how he reached the level he did in the time allotted. We wonder the more because of his lack of what we ordinarily call "advantages" (under which we can include such things as parental warmth, formal education, financial security, and, later on, health). We become still more interested because the use of the label "genius," as an easy way of resolving the problem of what leads men to greatness, is especially ineffective in the case of Keats. To use that word "genius" as a crutch is forgivable only in those highly technical or abstract pursuits (mathematics, for example, or—in the arts—music) where the talent that works in that particular, specialized medium invariably shows itself very early. It becomes increasingly naïve to grasp at it, as a crutch, when we move into the more open-ended activities (statesmanship, the empirical sciences, the broader uses of literature), where *experience* and its creative use by an experiencing nature become indispensable. Keats was not even precocious, in any usual sense of the word. He did not even try to write poetry, as far as we know, before the age of eighteen or nineteen; and what he first wrote—what he continued, for that matter, to write before he was twenty-one—is far from giving us any suggestion that he might become more than a middling poet. As we look a little more closely at his life, we begin to feel that—whatever else entered into the picture—the first gropings, then the increasingly rapid progress, are inseparable from certain qualities of character: courage (a virtue without which, as Aristotle said, we have little chance of practicing the other virtues), charity and sympathetic awareness of others, humor, good sense, and, above all, honesty—qualities of character constantly operating through an imagination at once steady, sane, clairvoyantly empathic, and humanly wayward. Because of this counterpoint of different qualities of character, it has been the unanimous verdict of critics and later poets that he possessed every sign of future growth—that he is, in effect, the most Shakespearean of poets, in general endowment. since Shakespeare himself.

Third, leaving aside, if we can, the personal drama of Keats's achievement—the extent to which it moves us to reconsider the basic educational problems, and the perennial questions of what permits or encourages human fulfillment—there remains, above all, the richly varied character of Keats's own writing, even if we think only of the poetry and neglect for the moment the famous letters ("certainly the most notable"—as T. S. Eliot says—"and the most important ever written by any English poet"). It is because of this variety that every generation has found something of value in his work. This is true not only of readers as a whole, or even critics and literary historians, but of poets, understandably severe in their views of predecessors.

Since the young Tennyson began to write (and, in America, since the time of James Russell Lowell), hardly any English-speaking poet worthy of the name, including even Whitman, has been uninfluenced by Keats. In addition, no poet since Milton has been more used as a direct model, and by more different kinds of poets, than Keats. The Pre-Raphaelites, in the late nineteenth century, with their interest in single pictures and the poetry of clean-cut *tableau,* could pluck out particular works and passages that struck them as models superior to what they could find in any other poet since the Renaissance. So with those Victorians who concentrated on the musical potentialities of poetry. Jumping to the twentieth century, many of the Edwardians followed what they considered a Keatsian mode (thinking especially of some of his sonnets); while, a little later, qualities similar to those prized by the Pre-Raphaelites were valued by the new Imagists, led by Amy Lowell, who viewed her large, warm-hearted biography of Keats as the climax of her career.

But the major poets, including those of the twentieth century (especially Eliot, Yeats, even Frost), have been more general—yet also more immediately personal—in what they have gained from Keats. What especially intrigues the practicing poet is, first of all, how Keats managed to extricate himself so quickly from so many of the stock responses of his own time about poetry, from the prevailing modes with which he grew up (in Keats's case a rampant sentimentalism), and from the restricted technical approaches that went along with this interest (for this is something every major poet has to achieve, as a rule only after a lifetime's effort); and, secondly, how he managed, in the course of only two years and a half (from late 1817, when he had just turned twenty-two, until the autumn of 1819, when he was approaching the age of twenty-four), to develop as many different styles of poetry as he did. For he created abundantly, and not merely year by year but almost by half and ultimately by quarter years. As he moved from the poems written in 1816, when he became twenty-one, through *Endymion* (when he was nearing twenty-two), to the great Miltonic fragment of *Hyperion,* written as he turned the age of twenty-three, his development was already constantly involving the creation of new styles. This in itself could lead us to feel that we are dealing with a fertility of invention inseparable from the quality we generally call *honesty.* Comparatively little of it seems to be the result of experimentation for its own sake. Still less can it be described as a search for novelty. (Keats, until he was twenty-three, was much too intoxicated with the example of the great poets of the past to desire anything more than to be as like them as possible; and even afterwards he was relatively free from the pressures toward originality and novelty that have been such a burden for the poet since the time of Dryden).

At almost every step we see that his overriding concern is a greater honesty to human experience, in its full concreteness, and in a search for greater fullness and richness of expression. After *Hyperion* the diversity of style increases and comes at a quicker pace. *The Eve of St. Agnes,* a respite from the more demanding effort of *Hyperion,* is rapidly followed by the fragment of *The Eve of St. Mark,* several minor poems, the ballad *La Belle Dame Sans Merci,* and then, in April and May, by the great odes, which may be said to begin the modern lyric of symbolic debate. Within three more months, though any number of personal difficulties arose, he turned from the odes to a still different poem, *Lamia,* while simultaneously creating still another new style of poetry in *The Fall of Hyperion.* Throughout Keats's final year of writing (the autumn of 1818 to the autumn of 1819), we are dealing with a development that takes place almost month by month and that, if spread over twenty years, would be a tribute to any poet's capacity for growth.

This is hardly the place to suggest the number of specialized ways in which this varied creativity has provided starting-points for later poetry (or at least anticipated it) from the Victorians down to the present day. But, in thinking of his final year of poetry, we can also say that no major poet was more vitally aware of the challenge before modern poetry *as it relates to* (and must someday be weighed in the balance against) the enormous, intimidating legacy of the past—Homer, Dante, Shakespeare, Milton, and all that the past exemplifies in what the English eighteenth century nostalgically called "the great *genres*," the greater forms of writing, especially the epic and the tragic drama. To follow Keats as he continues to educate himself through the greatest poetry of the past, and as he at the same time turns clairvoyantly to the next task before poetry (including the exploration of the inner life promised in the *Ode to Psyche*), has proved to be one of the most encouraging and cleansing experiences that the modern poet can have.

II

Our concern, in reprinting the selections that follow, is the mid-twentieth century approach to Keats. But we needed to preface these selections with at least a suggestion of why our present-day view of him does not (as in the case of many poets) dramatize a break with the past so much as it provides a deepening and enrichment of earlier attitudes. The mid-twentieth century has no quarrel—at least it should not have—with what Tennyson or even the Pre-Raphaelites valued in Keats. It need not even quarrel with late Victorian "art-for-art's-sake" writers who abstracted from him a sort of patron saint (and, because of his early death, a martyred saint). What these, and other values (or interests), relate to is very much a part of Keats.

But as we look back on the more run-of-the-mill interpretations of Keats until after World War I (there were always exceptions), we feel that they often missed the whole of the forest and concentrated on only a few trees. All of us look for what is uppermost in our minds—for what we ourselves most want or sometimes most fear to find—and, in plucking it out and stressing it, we naturally betray ourselves. As our knowledge of Keats grows and as we have seen him emerge more triumphantly with every change of taste, we naturally take a more comprehensive view, whatever our own hobbies and preoccupations. We also come to see his development as an artist more in relation to his general character. The essential manliness of Keats (his courage, openness, empathy, good sense) was already partly demonstrated in the first biography of him, that by Lord Houghton over a century ago (1848). But the original sources that Houghton himself used (though in a very fragmentary way) were almost completely neglected for fifty or sixty years; and very often the impression of Keats, in the late nineteenth century and even the early 1900s, was as more of a sensitive aesthete than he actually was.

The fine, comprehensive biography by Sir Sidney Colvin (1917) attempted a whole-scale reconsideration of Keats, and Colvin's book was closely followed by the two-volume biography by Amy Lowell (1925). Colvin, in his approach to poetic style, was naturally late Victorian and Edwardian in his premises, whereas Amy Lowell was a militant champion of the poetry of her time. Another difference is that Colvin was a more cautious scholar in his use of biographical data, while Miss Lowell, who was not a practiced scholar, was often dazzled by the paraphernalia of scholarship and tended to be impetuous and occasionally one-eyed in her use of it as well as in her emotional speculations. But these important books, coming so close together, did more than anything else to provide a capacious and indeed a most valuable source for those poets and critics who instinctively felt that at least a part of what Keats wrote was relevant to their own interests. This was true even though the great revival of metaphysical poetry, led by T. S. Eliot, was well underway by the mid-1920s, and though that revival brought with it so impatient a rejection of other writers of the nineteenth century. John Middleton Murry's important *Keats and Shakespeare* (1925) served as a further rallying point for several critics and poets. Meanwhile, Professor John Livingston Lowes of Harvard, remembered especially for his great source-study of Coleridge, *The Road to Xanadu,* was encouraging a dozen young scholars a year to concentrate on Keats, while he himself planned a major work on Keats's sources (a work never finished). Merely to list the names of Lowes's students is to summarize much of the critical and scholarly work on Keats written during the 1920s and 1930s, but of special interest is, first of all, the magisterial study of Keats in relation to his sources by Claude Finney, in his two-volume *Evolution of Keats's Poetry* (1936). The year following Finney's book saw the publication of what has long been a standard work, *Mythology and the Romantic Tradition* (1937), by a former student of Lowes, Douglas Bush—a work that has helped to establish its author as an authority to authorities (and in other periods besides that of the romantics). Amy Lowell's great collection of Keats had meanwhile come to Harvard after her death (1925), and was later to be supplemented by the collection that had been made, almost a century before, by Lord Houghton. Working with these manuscripts, and closely studying Keats's revisions, M. R. Ridley of Oxford brought out his *Keats's Craftsmanship* (1937). Also working with the manuscripts, in America and England,

H. W. Garrod produced his authoritative edition of the *Poems* (1939). Throughout these years, one of the three or four greatest Keats scholars and critics of the past half century, Professor Clarence Thorpe of the University of Michigan, directed and counseled teachers, biographers, and critics. His own pioneer work, *The Mind of John Keats* (1926), illustrates the way in which intrinsic gifts of character (especially sympathetic imagination) are themselves indispensable to the critic in approaching a great writer. During the war years and afterwards, Hyder Edward Rollins brought out one of the great source books for Keats scholars, the two-volume *Keats Circle* (1948), later followed by his definitive edition of Keats's *Letters* (1958).

The period since World War II, in its still growing interest in Keats, may be said to continue and to lend nuances to the insights (and the attempts to consolidate insights) of the 1920s and 1930s. Students of Douglas Bush, Clarence Thorpe, and Hyder Rollins have explored critically every aspect of Keats's life and work. In fact a special periodical has been founded (the *Keats-Shelley Journal*) in order to supplement the abundant critical and scholarly contributions that appear every year, while an older periodical abroad (the *Keats-Shelley Memorial Bulletin*) continues to be published.

III

Meanwhile, in the more special field of criticism itself, the interest in Keats has spread to every aspect of his poetry—imagery, the uses of symbol and metaphor, verse-pattern and verbal music, predominant themes, his relation to the history of ideas, the gradual evolution of his own ideas, and, more generally, the relation of Keats to the mid-twentieth century effort in poetry.

The selections printed below are offered with the hope of representing, in a fairly broad way, the current attempt to reconsider Keats's poetry. Naturally a great deal has had to be omitted, in this cramped space, that could be argued as being indispensable.

Biographical interpretations (which need far more room than we have in which to present themselves) have regretfully had to be omitted, especially since the assigned subject of these selections is "critical commentary" on the writer's works and thought.

Discussions of Keats's poetry that work organically, through a broad context, and would thus necessitate in most cases a number of pages at least equal to this entire book, have also had to be omitted. (Thorpe's *The Mind of John Keats* and Murry's *Keats and Shakespeare** are two examples.)

Some attention naturally had to be given to the chronological spread of Keats's own work, and to selecting critical discussions that would touch on these different works. Otherwise the volume might have consisted primarily of critical discussions of only three or four poems.

In any case, the point to be emphasized is the breadth and richness of our contemporary commentary on Keats's poetry—our continued reconsideration of it, progressively more active with every decade since the middle of the nineteenth century, until the quality that now most interests us is that which we associate with only the greatest writers—his universality.

* It was my hope to include one of the separate essays from another volume by the late Mr. Murry. Because of copyright complications, it was not possible to do so until after the present collection had gone to press. I have therefore ventured to insert, in place of it, an excerpt from a discussion of my own ("Negative Capability").

I

General Discussions

Keats

by T. S. Eliot

Keats seems to me also a great poet. I am not happy about *Hyperion*: it contains great lines, but I do not know whether it is a great poem. The Odes—especially perhaps the *Ode to Psyche*—are enough for his reputation. But I am not so much concerned with the degree of his greatness as with its kind; and its kind is manifested more clearly in his Letters than in his poems; and in contrast with the kinds we have been reviewing, it seems to me to be much more the kind of Shakespeare.[1] The Letters are certainly the most notable and the most important ever written by any English poet. Keats's egotism, such as it is, is that of youth which time would have redeemed. His letters are what letters ought to be; the fine things come in unexpectedly, neither introduced nor shown out, but between trifle and trifle. His observations suggested by Wordsworth's *Gypsey,* in a letter to Bailey of 1817, are of the finest quality of criticism, and the deepest penetration:

"It seems to me that if Wordsworth had thought a little deeper at that moment, he would not have written the poem at all. I should judge it to have been written in one of the most comfortable moods of his life—it is a kind of sketchy intellectual landscape, not a search for truth."

And in a letter to the same correspondent a few days later he says:

> In passing, however, I must say one thing that has pressed upon me lately, and increased my Humility and capability of submission—and that is this truth—Men of Genius are great as certain ethereal chemicals operating on the Mass of neutral intellect—but they have not any individuality, any de-

[1] I have not read Mr. Murry's *Keats and Shakespeare*: perhaps I say no more than Mr. Murry has said better and more exhaustively in that book; I am sure that he has meditated the matter much more deeply than I have.

termined character—I would call the top and head of those who have a proper self Men of Power.[2]

This is the sort of remark, which, when made by a man so young as was Keats, can only be called the result of genius. There is hardly one statement of Keats about poetry, which, when considered carefully and with due allowance for the difficulties of communication, will not be found to be true; and what is more, true for greater and more mature poetry than anything that Keats ever wrote.

But I am being tempted into a descant upon the general brilliance and profundity of the observations scattered through Keats's letters, and should probably be tempted further into remarking upon their merit as models of correspondence (not that one should ever take a model in letter-writing) and their revelation of a charming personality. My design, in this very narrow frame, has been only to refer to them as evidence of a very different kind of poetic mind than any of those I have just been considering. Keats's sayings about poetry, thrown out in the course of private correspondence, keep pretty close to intuition; and they have no apparent bearing upon his own times, as he himself does not appear to have taken any absorbing interest in public affairs—though when he did turn to such matters, he brough to bear a shrewd and penetrating intellect. Wordsworth had a very delicate sensibility to social life and social changes. Wordsworth and Shelley both theorise. Keats has no theory, and to have formed one was irrelevant to his interests, and alien to his mind. If we take either Wordsworth or Shelley as representative of his age, as being a voice of the age, we cannot so take Keats. But we cannot accuse Keats of any withdrawal, or refusal; he was merely about his business. He had no theories, yet in the sense appropriate to the poet, in the same sense, though to a lesser degree than Shakespeare, he had a "philosophic" mind. He was occupied only with the highest use of poetry; but that does not imply that poets of other types may not rightly and sometimes by obligation be concerned about the other uses.

[2] Mr. Herbert Read quotes this passage in his *Form in Modern Poetry,* but pursues his speculations to a point to which I would not willingly follow him.

Keats

by Douglas Bush

Keats is probably the only romantic poet, apart from Blake, whose present rank is conspicuously higher than it was in the nineteenth century, and the rank given him by critics and poets of that period was not low. What is there in Keats that has enabled him to emerge from modern scrutiny a larger figure than ever before? In the first place, he carries relatively little excess baggage in the way of mediocre writing or "dated" ideas from which, in various ways and degrees, Wordsworth, Coleridge, Byron and Shelley must be cut loose. Keats speaks to us directly, almost as one of ourselves; we do not need to approach him through elaborate reconstructions of dead philosophies or dead poetical fashions. The romantic elements in him remained, so to speak, central, sane, normal—in everything but their intensity—and did not run into transcendental or pseudoromantic or propagandist excesses. It is one of Keats's essential links with some poetic leaders of our own age that he, alone among the romantic poets, consciously strove to escape from self-expression into Shakespearean impersonality.

Moreover, there is nowadays a much more general understanding of the solid strength of Keats's mind and character, of his philosophic attitude toward life and art, of his astonishing self-knowledge and capacity for growth, of his unceasing struggle to achieve poetic integrity. In all these respects, and especially in the last, he is linked with the serious poets of the present. Certain fundamental questions are always tormenting him; he can neither put them aside nor finally answer them. Has the artist a right to exist at all in the midst of chaos and wrong and suffering? If his existence is justified, can he allow his imagination to be self-centered, in the large sense "lyrical," or should it be dramatic and rooted in the heart

"Keats." From *Mythology and the Romantic Tradition* (Cambridge, Mass.: Harvard University Press, 1937) by Douglas Bush. The Chapter on Keats has been considerably shortened by the author, and most of the footnotes omitted, especially for the present volume.

of man and human life? Is truth, the truth which is the soul of poetry, to be won by sensuous intuition or by study and conscious thought? From first to last Keats's important poems are related to, or grow directly out of, these inner conflicts, conflicts which are all the more acute because his poetic ambitions are so often at odds with his poetic gifts. This central problem has been expounded many times of late years, but, in a chapter which necessarily reviews a large part of Keats's work, one can hardly take hold of any other thread.

I

The *Ode to Apollo* (1815) may be taken as an illustration of one of his youthful eighteenth-century phases. It is not at all an ode in the richly meditative and introspective manner, but an objective declamatory sketch of the progress of poesy like many earlier imitations of the odes of Gray, Collins, and others on poetry, music, and kindred themes. In most of the poem Keats is only practising a worn-out convention, echoing the phrases of Dryden and Thomson, Gray and Beattie, but in the best lines, the first two, there is a gleam of mythological fancy:

> In thy western halls of gold
> When thou sittest in thy state . . .

These lines have caught richer echoes, from Jonson's *Queen and huntress* and Collin's *To Evening*:

> O Nymph reserv'd, while now the bright-hair'd Sun
> Sits in yon western Tent . . .

Keats's first line is a faint anticipation of "the realms of gold" and "western islands." The young bard's fealty to Apollo is as yet only a verbal inheritance; the deeper meaning it acquired during the next four years was to be set forth in *Hyperion.*

The Epistle *To George Felton Mathew* (November, 1815) is one of Keats's early poems of escape. His physical orbit is restricted to the Borough, and his increasingly irksome medical studies prevent his mind from flying away to nature and poetry:

> But 'tis impossible; far different cares
> Beckon me sternly from soft "Lydian airs,"

And hold my faculties so long in thrall,
That I am oft in doubt whether at all
I shall again see Phoebus in the morning:
Or flush'd Aurora in the roseate dawning!
Or a white Naiad in a rippling stream;
Or a rapt seraph in a moonlight beam.

This is apparently Keats's first series of mythological allusions, and their quality is prophetic, however dimly, of his more mature manner. They are not merely eighteenth century tinsel, they are symbols of the sensuous joys of nature and poetry. Nature and poetry, poetry and myth, are one. Further, the poem contains the first embryonic statement of Keats's conflicting poetic impulses, though as yet they are scarcely in conflict. The more immediate pleasures are those of the eye and the realm of sense, but he goes on to speak of humanity, of the harsh treatment accorded poets, whose genius has helped to cure the stings of the pitiless world; and, as a good disciple of Clarke and "Libertas," he celebrates great champions of national freedom. The epistles addressed to George Keats and Clarke (August and September, 1816) show a similar mixture of themes and motives, from maidens with breasts of cream to the inevitable Alfred and William Tell. Sensuous delights and humanitarian aspirations follow one another in wayward alternation—the scarlet coats of poppies even suggest the pestiferous soldiery—and, though the two poetic worlds are not set in opposition, there is no doubt which is the more instinctive and congenial.

I Stood Tip-toe (1816) is the work of a young man who is literally in a transport of sensuous intoxication. At first sight the poem may appear only "a poesy of luxuries," sometimes described, however, with a new, sure delicacy and even largeness of expression, but the essential thing is Keats's first full affirmation of the identity of nature, myth, and poetry; hence the significance of the allusions to Psyche, Pan, Narcissus, and particularly Endymion and Cynthia, for the poem was, we remember, a first attempt on the theme of *Endymion.* Keats writes of Narcissus, for instance, almost as if he had himself invented the myth while gazing into a Hampstead pond, and when one thinks of his progressive adaptation of myth to humanitarian symbolism one may say, by way of definition, not disparagement, that he is as yet a self-centered Narcissus. These allusions are mostly in Keats's early vein of sugary softness, though the passage on Cynthia contains some pure, clear beauty, but they are not merely ornamental. His boyish passion for myth had been confirmed, as instinct ripened into understanding, by the potent authority of Wordsworth, whose inspiring discourse on mythology in *The Excursion* was a fundamental chapter in Keats's poetic bible. Yet the identifying of nature and myth had been, so to speak, incidental in Wordsworth. He was glad to find in the origins of myth a traditional and religious sanction for his own natural religion, but the element of pure myth was far less important to him than to Keats; he had deliberately excluded it from most of the poetry by which he lives. Wordsworth did not, until his inner vision faded, see a dryad behind every oak tree; he had little of Keats's half-sophisticated, half-primitive delight in the sheer beauty of mythological tales. And, so preoccupied was Wordsworth in philosophizing what he saw, one may doubt if he was able to surrender himself so completely and ecstatically to the beauty of nature for its own sake, if he could become, as Keats could, a stalk of waving grain.

For a better parallel, in some respects, one must go back to Spenser, because, even if he did not view nature with modern romantic eyes, Spenser more than any other English poet had equated poetry and myth, had used myth for both decoration and symbol. Keats is commonly linked with the Elizabethans by virtue of his sensuous richness, but there are less obvious and not less important links than that. For one thing, in Keats as in a number of Elizabethans, it is almost impossible to draw a line between sensuous and spiritual experience. For another, Keats was the only one among the romantic poets who could quite naturally accept and carry on the allegorical interpretation of myth as he found it in Spenser, Chapman, Sandys, and others; of course he does not, with medieval and Elizabethan "naïveté," understand mythology in literal religious, ethical, and scientific applications, but he is, by instinct and influence, in the same tradition. Like Spenser, too, he loves beauty in its concrete and human forms, and sees in myth a treasury of the "material sublime." Though Cynthia, in *I Stood Tip-toe,* brings him "Shapes from the invisible world," Keats is happier among visible things.

In *Sleep and Poetry,* written in the autumn and winter of 1816, his contradictory impulses and ambitions reveal the beginnings of genuine conflict. The exposition of the three stages of poetic development, taken over from *Tintern Abbey* (and later paralleled, with deeper understanding, in the letter on the mansion of life) , leads from the glad animal movements of the carefree schoolboy through the adolescent passion for the finer joys of nature and sense. Keats's symbols for this passion, however, are not the cataract, the rock, the mountain and the wood, but the realm of Flora and old Pan, and kisses won from white-shouldered nymphs.

It is in this world, amid this store of luxuries, that he is now delightedly dwelling. The third stage, partly retrospective for Wordsworth, is for Keats an anticipation of the future, and he almost has to goad himself on. He "must pass" these joys for a nobler kind of poetry, that which deals with the agonies, the strife of human hearts. The poem has all the varieties of style that we expect in Keats's earlier work, from the Titianesque Bacchus and the pretty descriptions of Hunt's pictures to the sculptural massiveness of "might half slumb'ring on its own right arm." In *Venus and Adonis* Shakespeare's Ovidian and Italianate mythology is only tapestry in comparison with the dew-bedabbled hare, the lark, and the snail, and in *Sleep and Poetry* the picture of Diana bathing is far inferior to that of the sea, which Keats had lately beheld with his own eyes, and the weeds that "Feel all about their undulating home." [1] Our old friends Alfred and Kosciusko appear, for a moment, sandwiched between Sappho and Petrarch and Laura, for in Keats's heart liberty is a noble but somewhat remote and chilly ideal compared with love. His desire to interpret sterner themes is wholly sincere, yet, for a poet untried by life, it is less strong than ardent youthful instinct for "the most heart-easing things."

No English poet has drawn more authentic inspiration from sculpture, painting, and literature, all of which are a part of "life," than Keats, and the sonnet "On an engraved gem of Leander" (March, 1816 or 1817) was an early proof of his gift for indirect description of a work of art, description which is the concentrated imaginative re-creation of both physical fact and human feeling. As for the sonnet on Chapman's *Homer,* or rather, on the discovery of a new imaginative world and the discovery by a poetic aspirant of his own genius, that can only be mentioned here, even though it started from ancient myth, the Homeric account of the wreck of Odysseus.

II

The masculine and classic style of the sonnet on Chapman was not recaptured until Keats wrote *Hyperion,* and that poem's monumental grandeur is of a different kind. It was hardly to be expected that he should rid himself all at once of some congenital faults of taste and certain baneful literary influences, both Elizabethan and contemporary. The manner of *Endymion* is largely that of *I Stood Tip-toe* and *Sleep and*

[1] Cf. Tennyson (*Merlin and Vivien,* 1. 230): "The blind wave feeling round his long sea-hall"; and *Iliad,* xiv. 16.

Poetry, luscious, half feminine, and often beautiful. There is a distinct growth in craftsmanship, but perhaps even more remarkable is the increased depth and breadth of his philosophic apprehension of myth. . . .

The poem has several though related meanings, and Keats's apparent intentions do not always seem to be in accord with the poetic result. The design of the whole is an organic unit, but the control of particular parts is uncertain, partly because Keats was a young and undisciplined artist, and partly because *Endymion* was a confessional poem growing out of immediate turmoil of spirit. Up to the last moment the hero is subject to conflicting desires and impulses, as his creator was to the end of his short life. And in addition to difficulties in the conscious exposition of inner conflict, there are unconscious implications, so that at times what is said in the lines seems to be partly contradicted by what can be read between them. *Endymion* was Keats's most serious early attempt to answer fundamental questions about the relation of the artist to his art and to the world. Shelley had asked similar questions in *Alastor,* and, without losing sight of other factors, one may perhaps understand *Endymion* best by taking it in part as a reply to Shelley, a reply which includes imitation and adaptation as well. Shelley's hero is a romantic idealist who finds no satisfaction in the unlovely world of humanity, and, frustrated in his quest, dies in solitude; but it is better, says Shelley, so to pursue the vision and perish than to live, a finished and finite clod, untroubled by a spark. No search for ideal love and beauty could be unattractive to Keats, and there is something of Shelley's hero in Endymion. Yet that hero, for all his powers of locomotion, inhabited, as Keats would see, an ivory tower. It is a fundamental source of Keats's strength, and of his hold upon us, that he, despite his love of poetic luxuries and devotion to art, shared and understood the common experience of mankind as Shelley, with all his humanitarian zeal, never did. Although, then, Endymion does not learn his lesson until the very end, his whole previous pilgrimage has been leading him away from purely visionary idealism to the knowledge that the actual world of human life must be accepted, not denied, and that only through participation in that life can the ideal be realized. That thoroughly Wordsworthian doctrine is, to be sure, the moral Shelley expounded in the preface to *Alastor* (which ends with some lines from *The Excursion*), but Shelley seems to have largely forgotten it in the poem, which is in effect a glorification of the unique and isolated visionary.

Before the appearance of his dream-goddess Endymion had been a contented devotee of Diana, who is the source and symbol of all particular manifestations of beauty, natural and artistic, sensuous and intellectual. But she is also the incentive to great deeds, since all our passions, as well as love, are, in their sublime, creative of essential beauty. Endymion's abandonment of active life and public service, and Peona's censure of such conduct, along with her brother's plea for the contemplative ascent to reality, reflect Keats's uncertain view of the predicament of the artist. Can writing poetry be included among the ways of doing good to the world? And, in poetry, what are the just claims of the senses and of humanity at large? When *Endymion* was passing through the press, Keats wrote to Taylor: "I have been hovering for some time between an exquisite sense of the luxurious and a love for Philosophy—were I calculated for the former I should be glad—but as I am not I shall turn all my soul to the latter." In this particular utterance there is no doubt which is Keats's primary instinct (however mistaken he is, for once, in his judgment of himself), but, as countless other utterances show, his sterner ambitions were fundamental and lasting. We may remember that by "philosophy" Keats means not so much philosophical and literary learning, though that is included, but "a comprehension (and a comprehension of a peculiar kind) of the mystery of human life." [2] He wanted to be Shakespearean, and the thought of all he could never be did not comfort him, it left him perpetually dissatisfied with what his special gifts enabled him to do best.

The dream-goddess seems, in Keats's intention, to represent the supreme aspect of ideal beauty which is ideal love; what he mainly describes is in fact the sensuous earthly passion which, at least in its earlier stages, brings torment with it. A major part of his plan is to show love progressing from selfish passion to spiritual altruism, but his instincts partly defeat his purposes; love does not, even in the case of the Indian maiden, rise so far as it should above the warm embracements of Endymion and his goddess and Venus and Adonis. When the goddess is an abstraction in the background, she is a chaste ideal Diana; when with her worshiper, she is more like Venus. As in *Alastor* the imagination of a young man and a poet cannot help presenting the ideal as a breathing, desirable woman rather than a principle of beauty. A deliberately colorless outline of the poem should have made clear, so far as an outline can, the consistently earthly and sensuous character of Endymion's passion. The staid Bailey deplored the "indelicacy," and wished that Keats had not been inclined toward "that abominable principle of Shelley!—that sensual love is the

[2] Murry, *Keats and Shakespeare,* p. 60.

principle of things." Though Miss Lowell's refusal to see symbolism in the poem was mere temperamental wrongheadedness, she did discern Keats's preoccupation with normal, youthful, amorous emotion. The dream-goddess is a symbol of the ideal, which Keats sincerely worshiped, but she is nine parts flesh and blood and one part Platonic. For Endymion, as for Philip Sidney, "Desire still cries, 'Give me some food,'" and he cannot, with high resignation, turn to a religious and philosophic second-best: "Leave me, O love which reachest but to dust."

To arrive at ideal friendship and finally love demands more than a sense of oneness with all nature and human story; sympathy for human suffering must be felt and actively displayed. Here, as critics have agreed, lies the significance of the episodes of Alpheus and Arethusa and Glaucus and the reviving of dead lovers. Glaucus's personal story is also a warning to Endymion, whose fancied disloyalty to his goddess is foreshadowed in Glaucus's desertion of Scylla for a sensual love. Moreover, although desirous of helping the distressed, Glaucus, like the hero of *Alastor,* had been reduced to impotence through a misguided passion which alienated him from mankind. If the dream-goddess had been kept wholly on the level of ideal love, the appearance of the Indian maiden would have been more logical; the goddess herself, however, comes so close to being a human love, except in her prolonged absences from her votary, that Keats might be said to have almost proved his case before the Indian maiden is introduced. But the episode makes the fourth book much clearer than the second and third. As Mr. Leonard Brown points out, the Arab maiden of *Alastor* was quite neglected by the hero, who had no thought for a mere human girl who loved him; but in Keats's parable the value of a human love must be made of central significance. While Shelley's self-centered poet found solitude and death, Endymion, in achieving selflessness, finds love and service and more abundant life.[3] Ideal love or beauty is a transcendent divinity not to be immediately apprehended by man, or by man isolated from his fellows; mortals can win that heaven only through intermediaries, through experience of human love and sympathy with sorrow. (The altruistic motive ought to govern this incident, but, in spite of the maiden's situation and her song, it is her beauty rather than

[3] There is another aspect of this annihilation of self. When Endymion exclaims that he has no self-passion, no identity, he is expressing the bewilderment of a soul drawn in opposite directions. But, since his quest symbolizes a poet's life, is he not here and elsewhere touching on that favorite idea of Keat's, the negative capability, the chameleon nature, of the artist, who has no real identity, no rigid self, but may be at one moment a sparrow picking about the gravel, at another Achilles shouting in the trenches?

her distress that seems to excite Endymion.) The idealist thinks that the abstract and the concrete, the spirit and the flesh, are remote from and opposed to each other, that in loving the Indian maiden he has forfeited his highest hopes. But, after much painful vacillation, he learns that apparent defeat was real victory, that earthly love and beauty are identical with the divine; he learns, in short, "the holiness of the Heart's affections and the truth of Imagination." This, a primary article in Keats's creed, we may if we like label as only another statement of the romantic doctrine of the beautiful soul, but Keats was too normal and sane to hold such a faith in any extravagant or half-spurious way; he wrote no *Epipsychidion*.

Thus, while Keats's hopes and confessions and beliefs are sometimes blurred and obscure, sometimes waywardly decorative, one can hardly fail to see the outlines of a large and really impressive symbolic plan. Nor, on the other hand, can one slight the earthly and sensuous emotions in order to keep a young poet on the plane of abstract or even humanitarian philosophizing. The Platonism of the poem, so far as it goes, is entirely sincere and fundamental, but, whatever he had absorbed from Spenser and others, there is little more in *Endymion* than an instinctive personal devotion to the ideal which is in some degree, like amorous passion, the birthright of any youthful poetic nature. Keats would not be what he is if he were not kindled by an authentic beam from the white radiance of the One, but his habitation is the dome of many-colored glass. He has grown immensely since *Sleep and Poetry,* where he had looked forth from the realm of Flora and old Pan to contemplate the agonies of human hearts, yet his humanitarian and Platonic faith, however sincere an affirmation, is still beyond his experience, and, in general, the more spiritual parts of the poem are less real than the sensuous. The harmony of the solution comes home to us less than the author's troubled and ever-present consciousness of discord. . . .

The last topic that can be touched is the incidental mythology, and two set pieces may be mentioned first, the *Hymn to Pan* and the *Ode to Sorrow*. The former was the most sustained good writing, and by far the richest mythological re-creation, that Keats had yet achieved. Some forced rhymes and other defects in detail are almost lost in the power of the whole. In the list of Pan's attributes Keats seems to be pouring out items gathered from a wide variety of reading—William Browne, Chapman, Spenser, John Fletcher, Sandys, Ben Jonson, Marston, and others—but there is mature art in the grouping and in the orchestration that mounts with such a grand crescendo to the last reverberating sounds. Wordsworth's grim, prim phrase, "A very pretty piece of Paganism," was not even true, for, as Colvin observed, the main "mystical" inspiration of the hymn came from Wordsworth himself. Keats's conception of Pan, however un-Greek, is in accordance with the allegorical tradition, but he so greatly enriches "the All" of the mythographers that his "Pan is, in fact, the symbol of romantic imagination, concrete in a thousand objective shapes, the very life itself of 'sensations rather than thoughts,' "[4] More deserving of Wordsworth's judgment is the somewhat irrelevant picture of the Bacchic procession in the fourth book, for that hardly does get beyond exotic and multitudinous color and ornament. But even if this is less satisfying than Keats's profounder treatments of myth, simply as a bravura piece it lives in the memory far more vividly than anything of Swinburne's.

Most of the incidental mythology is of course in Keats's early vein of Elizabethan luxuriance. Endymion's dream-goddess, when first described, seems to have more than the usual complement of lips and eyes, but the lines just following are better:

> Ah! see her hovering feet,
> More bluely vein'd, more soft, more whitely sweet
> Than those of sea-born Venus, when she rose
> From out her cradle shell. The wind out-blows
> Her scarf into a fluttering pavillion;
> 'Tis blue, and over-spangled with a million
> Of little eyes, as though thou wert to shed,
> Over the darkest, lushest blue-bell bed,
> Handfuls of daisies.

Keats's eye is in a sense on the object, and in his fresh enjoyment of physical beauty he forgets his symbolic theme; his goddess is soft white flesh. A parallel passage, in the chief work of Shelley's maturity, is at first a Botticellian picture of crystal purity and simplicity—though when he comes to love his canvas flares into a Turner sunrise—and Shelley's Asia or Venus is a symbol only. A similar contrast, though the theme is not mythological, appears in the two poets' descriptions of wrecks and ruins of time, where Shelley certainly remembered Keats.[5] Shelley's relics symbolize the powers of destruction which the millennium has made obsolete. Keats's list, partly Shakespearean, partly Virgilian,[6] seems to be inspired

[4] H. W. Garrod, *Keats* (Clarendon Press, 1926), p. 81.

[5] *Endymion,* iii. 123 ff.; *Prometheus Unbound,* IV. 287 ff.; *Letters of Shelley,* ed. Ingpen (1914), II, 829; Colvin, *John Keats,* pp. 239-40.

[6] See *Richard III,* I. iv. 24 ff.; *Aeneid,* vii. 183 ff.

mainly by the brevity and littleness of man's life and works; if he is thinking of symbols of human art his choice of items is rather confused. But of course Keats is not always concerned with the fact and Shelley with the thesis; the myth of Arethusa serves Keats for humanitarian symbolism and for Shelley means pure lyric ecstasy.

Much might be said about Keats's mixed sources, for he is as little of a purist in such matters as Chaucer or Spenser. And even if a myth remains "pure," he can distil the essence of romantic magic—"Aeaea's isle was wondering at the moon." To the unblinking objectivity of Ovid he adds warm human feeling, as in "Dryope's lone lulling of her child," or a depth of pictorial and emotional suggestion, as in the picture of Cybele or "blind Orion hungry for the morn." This last phrase, by the way, is one of those changes which make Keats's revisions an education in taste. But there are other poems to speak of and one must come to an end.

III

The sensuous, imaginative and fanciful *Endymion* expressed the first virgin passion of a soul communing with the glorious universe. During 1818 Keats began really to learn that "Sorrow is Wisdom." The removal of George and his wife, reviewers' mauling of *Endymion,* physical ailments aggravated by the Scottish tour, the stings of sexual passion (not yet concentrated on Fanny Brawne), and, finally, the fatal decline of Tom, all these things compelled Keats to seek a "feverous relief" in "abstract images," "those abstractions which are my only life." "Poor Tom—that woman—and Poetry were ringing changes in my senses." In such circumstances the long-planned *Hyperion* got under way. That poem must be held over until we reach the revised version. Meanwhile we may very briefly take stock of Keats's position in regard to "sensation" and "thought," and then consider the great group of odes.

If Shakespeare was always the deity in Keats's poetic heaven, Wordsworth and Milton were saints under the throne. Shakespeare was the very opposite of the egotistical sublime, the great exemplar of negative capability, of undogmatic, unobtrusive, impersonal art, but Wordsworth and Milton were more approachable and more imitable. Keats's vacillating allegiance to these two poets is one of the clearest testimonies to the conflict in himself, the conflict he discerned in Milton, between the ardors and the pleasures of song. The letters record so many changes of attitude, so many fluctuating moods, sometimes ripples on the surface, sometimes not, that it is difficult to generalize,[7] but, with reservations, it may be said that when Wordsworth is in the ascendant Keats's mind and poetic ambition are turned to the human heart, the mysteries of pain and existence, the improvement of the world; and the ascendancy of Milton, though he sometimes appears as a humanitarian and champion of liberty, means that Keats is enjoying great art and fine phrases with the passion of a lover. But this is all a matter of emphasis and shading, not a clear-cut division. Keats was always striving for unity; in *Endymion* he had attempted to unite the ideal and the real, and in the two *Hyperions* he was to do so again. Where the odes stand in relation to that problem we may try to see.

The fragmentary *Ode to Maia* (May, 1818), and *To Autumn* (September, 1819), the first and the last of the great odes, stand apart in mood as well as in chronology from the group written in the spring of 1819. These two, in their pure, untroubled sensuousness, their objective directness and simplicity of feeling and expression, their lack of "spirituality," form, as it were, a serene frame for a troubled picture. *To Autumn* lies outside our range, though the delicate personifications of the second stanza exhibit Keats's myth-making instinct at its ripest and surest. The initial literary impulse for the *Ode to Maia* may have come from Barnabe Barnes's ode "Lovely Maya," but Keats is not here writing like an Elizabethan or like his earlier self; for a more lush and uneven handling of a similar theme one might compare the dedication of the 1817 volume. Instead of the exuberant catalogue of nature and myth and the Wordsworthian symbolism of the *Hymn to Pan,* the *Ode to Maia* is content with the quiet primrose and the simple worship of a day; we may remember what Severn liked to remember, Keats's talk about Greek polytheism as a "religion of joy." The poem is as Greek in its sober simplicity of expression as it it un-Greek in its pure romantic nostalgia. And it takes its place among Keats's affirmations on the side of the senses.[8]

[7] For instance, on January 23, 1818 (*Letters,* Oxford [1935], p. 86), Keats copies the poem on Milton he had written two days before; in it he longs to "grow high rife with Old Philosophy." A month later (p. 104), in the lines on the thrush sent to Reynolds, he says: "O fret not after knowledge . . ."; he has none, and can sing as well without it. Two days later (p. 107) he is reading Voltaire and Gibbon, although he "wrote to Reynolds the other day to prove reading of no use."

[8] See the discussion in the letter of May 3 which contains the poem (*Letters,* pp. 140-41).

Students have sometimes wondered what connection there was between Maia and Baiae. In Lempriere (1804 ed.) there is a note on "Maiama, festivals in honor of Maia, celebrated on the first of May among the Romans," and it is said that "the principal inhabitants frequented Ostia to spend their time in greater festivity." Keats might have

The *Ode to Psyche* is the least coherent and most uneven of the later group. The author of *Endymion* reveals himself in such phrases as "fainting with surprise" and "tender eye-dawn of aurorean love," and in the too lavish decoration. But it is only in comparison with himself that Keats suffers, and there is no lack of the magic with which he units myth, nature, and literature. Psyche has not, like Maia, been rich in the simple worship and happy pieties of ancient times. Latest born of the faded hierarchy, she has had no priest or choir, no music or incense; only the poet can celebrate her now. The poem does not embody the traditional allegory of Cupid and Psyche. Keats's branched thoughts are far removed from the spirit of Milton's mystical allusion at the end of *Comus;* he is contemplating, not the Bride of the Lamb, but soft delight and warm love. And "Yes, I will be thy priest" is equally far from "Make me thy lyre, even as the forest is." The west wind of liberty is characteristic of the whole of Shelley; Keats's symbols are characteristic of that half of his mind which found its finest expression in these odes.

At first sight Keats's theme in the *Ode to a Nightingale* and the *Ode on a Grecian Urn*—the two cannot be separated—is the belief that whereas the momentary experience of beauty is fleeting, the ideal embodiment of that moment in art, in song, or in marble, is an imperishable source of joy. If that were all, these odes should be hymns of triumph, and they are not. It is the very acme of melancholy that the joy he celebrates is joy in beauty that must die. Even when Keats proclaims that the song of the bird is immortal, that the sculptured lover feels an enduring love that is beyond the pains of human passion, his deepest emotions are fixed on the obverse side of his theme. He tries to believe, and with part of his mind he does believe and rejoice, in the immortality of ideal beauty, but he is too intense a lover of the here and now, of the human and tangible, to be satisfied by his own affirmations. It is the actual moment that is precious, that brings ecstasy with it, and the moment will not stay. The truth that Keats embraces is not that of his large humanitarian aspirations, nor the smaller measure of truth granted to the philosophic intellect, it is the truth, that is, the reality, apprehended through the senses. The author of these odes hears the still, sad music of humanity, but he tries to escape from it. The bird's song, poetry, carries him away from the lazar-house of life and above the level of the dull, perplexing brain; the

---

confused Ostia with Baiae, or might have substituted the latter name for the sake of meter and rhyme (however bad the rhyme). This note is not in the 1806 edition of Lempriere, the one now at the Keats House, but, as Mr. Forman remarks (*Letters*, p. 513), Keats apparently had two copies in his time.

urn is a symbol of untroubled beauty in the midst of human woe and it teases him out of thought. Was it the ecstasies and torments of love that intensified and decided the conflict, or was it that in poetry the senses had for the time won the victory and released him from the half-paralyzing claims of "higher" poetry? At any rate, as in *Endymion,* Keats is not wholly happy with the ideal, his instinct seeks the particular object and experience. And his instincts are more honest than Shelley's, for he is always aware of the cleavage in himself. He may grasp at the ideal as an authentic and inspiring sanction for his love of the actual, but he does not deceive himself, or us, when he endeavors, with more than Shelley's occasional misgivings, to bridge the gap between them. He cannot so easily rhapsodize about Intellectual Beauty when he is thinking of holding the hands of Harriet or Mary or Emilia or Jane. Neither beauty nor truth is for Keats a real abstraction, a Platonic Idea; beauty is something beautiful, the "material sublime." When he tries to generalize from a melancholy ecstasy, he remains at odds with himself. The urn is a joy for ever, but the marble figures are cold.

Probably no one but William Michael Rossetti has found in the *Nightingale* "a surfeit of mythological allusions." They are all so harmonious that one may forget they are there. Keats's taste in the matter of allusions is generally that of the Elizabethans and Jacobeans from whom he drew so much of his mythology. Quite Elizabethan, too, is his mingling of classical and native lore; Diana, the queen-moon, is "Cluster'd around by all her starry Fays." Many readers of the *Grecian Urn* have wondered, no doubt, if Keats had ever heard Sidney's shepherd's boy "piping, as though he should never be old,"[8] but he must have known William Browne's echo of Sidney.[9] And, without forgetting the Elgin Marbles, several urns, and Claude's painting, one may add a bit from Sandys' *Ovid* to the citations given by Mr. De Selincourt; Cadmus followed a heifer which

> made a stand; to heaven her fore-head cast,
> With loftie horns most exquisitely faire;
> Then, with repeated lowings fill'd the ayre.[10]

But of course no array of parallels is of much account. When Keats mixes

[9] Sidney's *Arcadia,* ed. A. Feuillerat (Cambridge University Press, 1912), p. 13; *Britannia's Pastorals,* Book ii, Song 2, ll. 33-36. The lines are quoted in *P.M.L.A.,* L, 803.

[10] Ed. 1640, p. 47. All the items of the similar sacrifice in the *Epistle to Reynolds* (ll. 20 ff.) are mentioned or suggested in Potter's *Archaeologia Graeca* (I, 251-73, especially 267-68). See Colvin, pp. 264, 416-17; De Selincourt, p. 586.

three sounds in his thought they become, not a fourth sound, but a star. The lines on the little town were quoted, or rather misquoted, by Arnold and praised for being Greek, "as Greek as a thing from Homer or Theocritus . . . composed with the eye on the object, a radiancy and light clearness being added." [11] But, as in the *Ode to Maia,* the concrete details are suffused with a rich nostalgia. The hard edges of classical Greek writing are softened by the enveloping emotion and suggestion. In his classical moments Keats is a sculptor whose marble becomes flesh.

IV

Keats was so right in his self-criticism that one hesitates to question any of his judgments, yet few modern readers seem to like *Lamia* as well as he did. It contains a great deal of sumptuous and admirable writing (along with some strange lapses), it shows a mastery of the couplet[12] and of coherent story-telling, and yet it is in essential ways the least satisfying of the longer poems. On the purely literary side *Lamia* is too much of a brilliant piece of tapestry. But the fundamental defect is that the poem has no emotional and philosophic unity. Clearly the story is not told merely for the story's sake, though the amount of ornament and the over-elaboration of the initial episode of Hermes might suggest that it is.[13] Whether or not it was his original intention, Keats gave the poem a meaning, so that it takes its place among the many poems which embody the inward struggle between the claims of self and the senses and the claims of the world and "philosophy." But here Keats does not seem to know which side he is on, and a plausible case can be, and has been, made out for *Lamia* as a condemnation of philosophy, as a condemnation of the senses, and as a condemnation of a divorce between the two. Each of these interpretations can be supported by chapter and verse from Keats's other poems and from his letters, yet each leaves difficulties in *Lamia* itself.

On the one hand Lamia is a sinister serpent woman; the house to which

[11] *On the Study of Celtic Literature and On Translating Homer* (New York, 1883), p. 125.

[12] The usual emphasis on the metrical influence of Dryden has been qualified by Mr. Ridley (pp. 241 ff.) and Mr. Charles A. Langworthy.

[13] This episode has been explained by Mr. Edward T. Norris as an integral part of the symbolism: "As Hermes represents the industrious poet in contrast to Lycius, the poet of sensation, so the nymph represents Keat's true ideal of poetry in contrast to Lamia, the poetry of sensation" (*ELH,* II [1935], 322-26). This seems to me quite unconvincing.

she takes her lover is a "purple-lined palace of sweet sin"; she is afraid when he hears the heroic sound of trumpets from the outside world, for she knows "that but a moment's thought is passion's passing bell." Such a conception is in general accord with the spirit of Burton's tale and his discussion of the destructive power of love; it is also in accord with two poems which probably had some influence on *Lamia,* namely, *Christabel* and *Rhododaphne.*[14] On the other hand Keats obviously sympathizes with the sensuous or sensual passion, the "unperplex'd delight," of the young lovers; Apollonius the sage is the ghost of folly haunting the sweet dreams of his former disciple; and at the end, when Apollonius is about to cast a blight upon Lamia, the author lets himself go in an attack on "cold philosophy." [15] Thus Lamia is at the same time a beautiful women who loves and should be loved, and a evil embodiment of the wasting power of love, a *belle dame sans merci.*

Such central contradictions cannot be reconciled. Spenser, with the easy flexibility of a Renaissance poet, could first exploit the sensuous and then condemn it; that compromise was impossible for Keats, a modern poet driven to seek for unity in himself and the world, yet we wonder, as we do in reading of the destruction of the bower of bliss, if Keats's stern conclusion expresses as much of himself as had gone into the tale of amorous enchantment. There is the essential difference, however, that Spenser was dealing largely with the world of imagination, as Keats was in *Endymion.* There Keats had arrived at a solution, a harmonizing of his instincts and his aspirations, yet the former element is so much the stronger, at that stage in the author's growth, that we doubt if the solution is final. The dilemma that faced Endymion, compared with that of Lycius, was esthetic and theoretical. The trouble in *Lamia* is that, despite the exotic story and trappings, the poem is a too immediate transcript of actual experience; despite the technical skill, it is, spiritually, the raw material of a poem. The conflict has been interpreted wholly in terms of poetry, of the senses and the intellect, and the attack on cold philosophy certainly belongs to poetic theory; it embodies not only one of Keats's own moods but

[14] In the sixth and seventh cantos of Peacock's poem we have the description of a rich palace erected by magic and a banquet room sumptuously arrayed, and the enchantress who has seduced the hero is destroyed by Uranian Love.

[15] It has been plausibly suggested (De Selincourt, p. 573) that in the line "Philosophy will clip an Angel's wings" Keats remembered Hazlitt's remark in the first of his *Lectures on the English Poets,* that "the progress of knowledge and refinement has a tendency to circumscribe the limits of the imagination, and to clip the wings of poetry." The proverbial phrase occurs twice in Burton, a few pages before the story of Lamia (Bohn's Popular Library ed., III, 45-46), and in Dryden's *Theodore and Honoria* (l. 54) "Love had clipp'd his Wings."

something of the general romantic protest agaist a purely scientific view of the world. Yet the fire that Keats was aware of in *Lamia* was not merely born of opposed literary desires, however intense, it came from the divided soul of a lover. The struggle between passion and the craving to escape from passion is felt too keenly and rendered too literally—the literalness is that of Keats, not of D. H. Lawrence—to result in a unified, integrated poem. "The truth about the Lamia," as Mr. Murry says, "is that Keats himself did not know whether she was a thing of beauty or a thing of bale. He only knew that if he were to be deprived of her, he would die, which he did, in the poem and in fact." [16] We may be moved, if we are not put off by the glittering surface, but we are moved in much the same way as we are in reading the letters to Fanny Brawne, which are after all the best commentary on the poem.

Of the frequent beauty of the writing there is no room or need to speak. The magnificent allusion to Hermes as "the star of Lethe" drew a magnificent eulogy from Lamb. William Morris must have envied the mingled simplicity and richness of the lines,

> Men, women, rich and poor, in the cool hours,
> Shuffled their sandals o'er the pavement white.

Keats could never, with the alcoholic fluency of Porson, have hiccuped Greek like a Helot, but how near could Porson have come to this?

> Soft went the music the soft air along,
> While fluent Greek a vowel'd undersong
> Kept up among the guests. . . .

But random comment must give place to my ewe-lamb of research. *Lamia* is the only classical story Keats reworked which required definite information about ancient manners and furniture, and he naturally turned to the standard book on the subject, a book he owned himself, John Potter's *Archaeologia Graeca*. Virtually all of the material background and customs described in *Lamia* appear to be drawn, sometimes with verbal echoes, from Potter, and we may observe Keats's selective memory and

[16] *Keats and Shakespeare,* p. 159. Mr. Murry's discussion of the autobiographical element in *Lamia* is illuminating but goes too far, much farther than, for example, Lucien Wolff (*John Keats,* Paris [1911], pp. 539 ff.). It is odd that a critic who sees the essential inwardness of the poem so sympathetically should so externalize Keat's inward struggle as to see Charles Brown behind Apollonius. Apart from the lack of evidence (see John H. Roberts, *P.M.L.A.*, L, 550-61), to take Apollonius as representing anything but one side of Keats is to empty the poem of its significance.

imagination transforming the learned but pedestrian pages of his authority into the romantic glamor and opulence of the poem. There is space for only one example of the process.

> Of wealthy lustre was the banquet-room,
> Fill'd with pervading brilliance and perfume:
> Before each lucid pannel fuming stood
> A censer fed with myrrh and spiced wood,
> Each by a sacred tripod held aloft,
> Whose slender feet wide-swerv'ed upon the soft
> Wool-woofed carpets. . . .
> Twelve sphered tables, by silk seats insphered,
> High as the level of a man's breast rear'd
> On libbard's paws, upheld the heavy gold
> Of cups and goblets. . . .
> Thus loaded with a feast the tables stood,
> Each shrining in the midst the images of a God.

The relevant items from Potter may be lumped together:

> And the room wherein the entertainment was made, was sometimes perfumed by burning myrrh or frankincense, or with other odours.
> The form [of tables] was round, if we may believe Myrleanus in Athenaeus, who reports, that the ancient Greeks made their tables, and several other things, spherical. . . .
> . . . the beds covered with cloth or tapestry, according to the quality of the master of the house.
> They [the tables] were also adorned with plates of silver, or other metals, and supported by one or more feet, curiously wrought. . . . The most common support of these tables was an ivory foot, cast in the form of a lion, a leopard, or some other animal.
> . . . their cups were made of silver, gold, and other costly materials.
> It was customary to place the statues of the gods upon the table.[17]

But Potter was a doubtful source of inspiration, for Keats is at his best when he does not follow sources so closely. The sensuous beauties of

[17] Ed. Edinburgh (1818), II, 383, 376, 373, 377, 390, 376. The chief passages in *Lamia* which seem to be related to Potter are i. 317 ff., ii. 106 ff., 191 ff., 208, 215 ff., 241 ff. For details see *P.M.L.A.*, L., 785 ff.; a number of the items are quoted in Finney, II, 674-77.

The episode of Hermes seems to be elaborated from the story of Mercury, Herse, and Aglauros, at the end of the second book of the *Metamorphoses*, and the picture of Lamia as she withers away under the eye of the sage perhaps owes something to the punishment of Aglauros in the same Ovidian tale. The passages from Sandys (ed. 1640, pp. 31, 32) are quoted in *P.M.L.A.*, L, 789.

Lamia are too often indoor and artificial, too material and mundane, for a poet who has taught us how high and deep the senses can reach.

V

Hyperion was begun in the autum of 1818 and finished by April, 1819, In August and September, and, according to Charles Brown, in November and December, 1819, Keats was engaged in remodeling the fragment in the form of a vision, *The Fall of Hyperion*. The subject had been conceived at least as early as September, 1817, and a number of references in the later books of *Endymion,* not to mention the preface, show that the new project was considerably occupying Keats's thoughts. What had been called in September "a new Romance" is differently described in another letter to Haydon of January 23, 1818:

> In Endymion I think you may have many bits of the deep and sentimental cast—the nature of *Hyperion* will lead me to treat it in a more naked and Grecian Manner—and the march of passion and endeavour will be undeviating—and one great contrast between them will be—that the Hero of the written tale being mortal is led on, like Buonaparte, by circumstance; whereas the Apollo in Hyperion being a fore-seeing God will shape his actions like one.

The first half of the fragment at least reveals few lapses from the naked and Grecian manner. To say, as critics often do, that *Hyperion* is not Keats, that it is a splendid *tour de force,* seems rather idle; we do not find fault with *Paradise Lost* because it is not in the style of *Comus.* Of course Keats had, in Milton, a single dominating literary model, as Milton had not, and one may therefore, if one likes, regard *Hyperion* as derivative and artificial. But *Hyperion* and its complement are, in important respects, entirely original—*Paradise Lost* was likewise, though it absorbed a thousand tributaries—and they are the culmination of Keats's poetic progress, the last and greatest statement of his conflicting instincts and ambitions. In finally abandoning the *Fall,* which not only retained most of the old Miltonisms but added new ones, Keats was moved less by a distaste for the Miltonic manner than by deeper reasons. I shall not attempt to speak here of Milton's influence, for I have nothing to add to the many discussions of style and diction, story and structure. But one may mention a subtle lesson that Keats learned from Milton, and put greatly into practice, the "stationing" of figures which his notes on Milton show that he had studied.[18]

Along with Milton other influences contributed to the strength and massiveness which are such an astonishing change from the lush and fanciful luxuriance of *Endymion*. Landor, the master of the definite line, may have been one of those influences; we remember that Shelley had a passion for *Gebir,* though his own writing was hardly Landorian. When, for instance, the undefeated Titan moves "With stride colossal, on from hall to hall," we feel certain that Keats had Shakespeare in mind, but he may also have known Landor's "The parting Sun's gigantic strides." The results of Keats's familiarity with the Elgin Marbles are none the less important for not being precisely demonstrable. *Hyperion* contains a number of Egyptian allusions, and the vast bulk of the Titans, which suggests beings more primeval than Phidian, may owe something to Keats's interest in Egyptian statuary. Hyperion's palace, too, is more Egyptian, or at least oriental, than Greek; in some respects it resembles a glorified mosque. Finally, not the least important influence that helped to create a setting worthy of the Titans, "a Stonehenge of reverberance," was the huge, rugged masses of northern scenery. The change from the soft richness and sweetness of *Endymion* to the bare grandeur of *Hyperion* is partly the result of a change from the Isle of Wight and Oxford and Box Hill to the lake country and Scotland. In a letter from the north of June 27, 1818, Keats said: "I cannot think with Hazlitt that these scenes make man appear little. I never forgot my stature so completely—I live in the eye; and my imagination, surpassed, is at rest." These last phrases perfectly describe the purely esthetic experience of reading *Hyperion*.

Though *Hyperion* is completely his own, Keats, like Virgil and Milton, was often most original when refining the ore, or engraving the gold, of other poets. While Shakespearean influence ranges from the conception of Saturn to versification, the chief group of Shakespearean details is the list of evil omens, for which Keats would go as naturally to Shakespeare as Shakespeare went to Plutarch and others. Landor, Southey, and Sandys may all have contributed to that Miltonic turn:

> How beautiful, if sorrow had not made
> Sorrow more beautiful than Beauty's self.

[18] "But in no instance is this sort of perseverance more exemplified, than in what may be called his *stationing or statuary*. He is not content with simple description, he must station,—thus here we not only see how the Birds *'with clang despised the ground,'* but we see them *'under a cloud in prospect.'* So we see Adam *'Fair indeed, and tall—under a plantane'*—and so we see Satan *'disfigured—on the Assyrian Mount'* " (Works, ed. Forman, 1889, III, 28-29).

But I need not venture upon comments which Mr. Lowes will shortly render obsolete, and for the same good reason I shall not summarize what has so far been discovered about the special sources of Keats's classical material. The probable or possible sources are as heterogeneous as ever —Chapman's *Homer,* Sandys' *Ovid,* Hyginus, Hesiod, Ronsard, Davies' *Celtic Researches,* the *Arabian Nights, Vathek,* and other books. Like medieval and Elizabethan poets, Keats altered mythology freely, and he welcomed post-classical accretions that old stories had gathered in passing through many hands.[19] To mention one more topic which must be passed by, Keats was never a finer artist than when improving on himself; *Hyperion* is full of inspired revisions.

By Milton's time, indeed by Virgil's, the conventional mold of the heroic epic had become inadequate for the increasingly abstract themes of modern and philosophic poets. Whatever Keats originally had in mind, his final plan avoided epic battles by starting after the defeat of the Titans and referring to war only in allusive retrospect, a method in harmony with his poetic temper and with his symbolic conception of the subject; how he would have ended the poem we can only guess.[20] Yet his method, however wise and necessary, involved difficulties. The first two books are a series of magnificent sculptural friezes, but the figures can hardly be set moving. They seem to be too much a stage setting for Apollo, who first appears in the third book and whose significance does not become entirely clear until we turn to the *Fall.* The chief reason for the abandonment of *Hyperion* may well have been, as Mr. Abercrombie in particular has said, that Keats perceived his poem to be mainly facade, that his elaboration of a semi-Miltonic pattern, though grand in itself, was smothering his idea under decoration. He must have known as well as we do that for stately elevation and beauty the first two books had no

[19] In *The Indicator* of December 8, 1819, Hunt wrote thus of a friend whom he later identified as Keats: "Talking the other day with a friend about Dante, he observed, that whenever so great a poet told us any thing in addition or continuation of an ancient story, he had a right to be regarded as classical authority. For instance, said he, when he tells us of that characteristic death of Ulysses in one of the books of his Inferno, we ought to receive the information as authentic, and be glad that we have more news of Ulysses than we looked for." "More News of Ulysses," *The Indicator* (1820), I, 65; W. E. Peck, "Keats on Poet-Historians," *Books, New York Herald-Tribune,* October 16, 1927. Incidentally, in regard to the date of *The Fall of Hyperion,* it is perhaps of some interest to find Keats citing Dante in November or December, 1819.

[20] Mr. De Selincourt (p. 488) suggests that Apollo, after being confirmed in his supremacy by Jove, "would have gone forth to meet Hyperion who, struck by the power of supreme beauty, would have found resistance impossible." For Woodhouse's account of the original plan, which involved war and the dethronement of a number of Titans, see De Selincourt, p. 486.

superior or equal since Milton, but, to a man of Keats's poetic conscience, it would have meant more that he was not getting his theme expressed. When the poem takes a fresh start in the fragmentary third book, he seems determined to come to grips with his central story, to set forth his "message"; by that time, however, if the poem was to comprise four books, the architecture was so much out of proportion that Keats did not see his way to a satisfactory ending or recasting. Milton and Wordsworth had been the two poles of Keats's poetical orbit, and, to change metaphors, the wedding of Miltonic technique to Wordsworthian inwardness was almost bound to be an unequal union.

If *Endymion* was in the philosophic sense Keats's *Prelude, Hyperion* was his Excursion. Apollo, like Endymion, is John Keats. But the author of *Hyperion* has emerged from the chamber of maiden-thought. The untried idealism of *Endymion* has not weakened; it has, under the stress of realities, become stronger, sterner, less self-centered. The facts of death and love have been proved on the author's pulses. "Sensations" without knowledge have ripened and deepened into sensations with knowledge. Although the mere "poetical" beauty of the fragment is completely satisfying even now, when so much merely beautiful poetry has faded, description is not simply description; it carries a weight of magnanimity and compassion which the author of *Endymion* could not let have felt or expressed. And Keats has not, like the elder Wordsworth, cut himself off from some of his youthful and essential roots; even though Keats did not solve his problem, the two *Hyperions* represent the consummation of his growth.

As a poem of evolution *Hyperion* has both social and personal aspects. We no longer think of Keats as the one great poet of his time who turned away from a troubled present to find esthetic refuge in a romantic Middle Age or romantic Greece. Letters and poems alike bear ample witness to his critical interests in public affairs and the state of society and to his vigorous liberal opinions. The author of *Hyperion,* like Wordsworth and Shelley, was a child of revolutionary optimism, but while Wordsworth literally and poetically lived through the vicissitudes of the French Revolution, and Shelley was often a shrill doctrinaire on the platform, Keats was always an artist and viewed his world, so to speak, with the eyes of posterity. In *Hyperion* Keats's treatment of myth is more like Spenser's that Shelley's. Spenser had made the war of the gods and Titans the vehicle for his deepest thoughts and feelings about the riddle of the one and the many, the possibility of permanence in the midst of flux. From a world of medieval fixities, if I may repeat myself, he contemplated the melancholy spectacle of endless change, and he arrived at a compromise half Christian, half scientific, the doctrine that all things work out their own perfection under divine control, until the process of change shall give way to the changelessness of eternity. Keats was no "Godwin perfectibility Man," and in *Hyperion* his faith in progress was put in a way peculiarly his own. The Jupiter whom Shelley overthrows is a wholly evil embodiment of superstition, tyranny, and custom, whose reign must give way to the rule of universal love. Keats's Titans, though beneficent rulers of the world, must yield to a race of gods superior in beauty and magnanimity. However familiar the speech of Oceanus, it must be partly quoted:

> And first, as thou wast not the first of powers,
> So art thou not the last; it cannot be:
> Thou art not the beginning nor the end. . . .
>
> Then thou first-born, and we the giant-race,
> Found ourselves ruling new and beauteous realms.
> Now comes the pain of truth, to whom 'tis pain;
> O folly! for to bear all naked truths,
> And to envisage circumstance, all calm,
> That is the top of sovereignty. Mark well!
> As Heaven and Earth are fairer, fairer far
> Than Chaos and blank Darkness, though once chiefs;
> And as we show beyond that Heaven and Earth
> In form and shape compact and beautiful,
> In will, in action free, companionship,
> And thousand other signs of purer life;
> So on our heels a fresh perfection treads,
> A power more strong in beauty, born of us
> And fated to excel us, as we pass
> In glory that old Darkness: nor are we
> Thereby more conquer'd, than by us the rule
> Of shapeless Chaos. . . .
> . . . for 'tis the eternal law
> That first in beauty should be first in might.

The passage hardly needs corroboration, but one may quote two more personal bits of prose. In the important letter of May 3, 1818, Keats had compared Milton and Wordsworth in regard to their zeal for humanity and their knowledge of the human heart, and he had put Wordsworth first, not because of individual superiority but because of a general advance among mankind. "What is then to be inferr'd? O many things—

It proves there is really a grand march of intellect—, It proves that a mighty providence subdues the mightiest Minds to the service of the time being, whether it be in human Knowledge or Religion." On September 18, 1819, Keats wrote: "All civil[iz]ed countries become gradually more enlighten'd and there should be a continual change for the better." One might add some brief queries from *The Excursion* which epitomize a good deal of Wordsworth:

> Is Man
> A child of hope? Do generations press
> On generations, without progress made? [21]

If Keats's notion of the enlightened progress of the race is partly Wordsworthian, still more so is the ideal of individual progress summed up in the speech of Oceanus, the power to bear all naked truths and face circumstance with calm. All through *The Excursion* Wordsworth is pleading for self-discipline achieved through reason and the law of duty, and for the "pagan" Keats, Wordsworth's stoicism would be detachable from his Christian faith. The soul, says Wordsworth, craves a life of peace, "Stability without regret or fear," the central peace subsisting at the heart of endless agitation.[22] Possessions, opinions, passions change, but duty remains, "by the storms of circumstance unshaken." Reason is "A crown, an attribute of sovereign power," and a life of discipline may enable Age, "in awful sovereignty," to sit on a superior height, disencumbered from the press of near obstructions.[23] One may dismiss all this as Polonian moralizing and say that Keats had no such stuff in mind when he named *The Excursion* as one of the three things in the age to rejoice at. But one can hardly read *Hyperion* or the letters and not believe that the attaining of such stability of soul was a reality to him. Again I must limit myself to two inadequate scraps. "The best of Men have but a portion of good in them—a kind of spiritual yeast in their frames which creates the ferment of existence—by which a Man is propell'd to act and strive and buffet with Circumstance." "Circumstances are like Clouds continually gathering and bursting—While we are laughing the seed of some trouble is put into the wide arable land of events—while we are laughing it sprouts [it] grows and suddenly bears a poison fruit which we must pluck."

[21] *Excursion*, v. 465-67. Cf. vii. 999 ff.
[22] *Ibid.*, iii. 385-86, iv. 1146-47.
[23] *Ibid.*, iv. 69-73, v. 503, ix. 55, 70. Cf. iv. 1070 ff., 1266 ff.

The words of Oceanus are no incidental exhortation, they cast back to the speech of Coelus in the first book, and they are essential to Keats's whole conception of the Titans and the significance of their defeat. He does not think of them as primitive deities of brute force and tyranny. Saturn laments that he is

> buried from all godlike exercise
> Of influence benign on planets pale,
> Of admonitions to the winds and seas,
> Of peaceful sway above man's harvesting,
> And all those acts which Deity supreme
> Doth ease its heart of love in.

Even Enceladus gives similar testimony.[24] The myth of a steady decline from the golden age is not for Keats. The Titans are superior to their predecessors; they are one link, not the first, in the upward succession. Indeed the principal Titans are so completely majestic and sublime that Keats would have been sorely tried in creating gods who could win our sympathy away from them. But his intention is clear. The Titans, however benign and beneficent, had in a crisis behaved not like deities but like frail mortals; they had lost, and deserved to lose, the sovereignty of the world because they had lost the sovereignty over themselves.

> Divine ye were created, and divine
> In sad demeanour, solemn, undisturb'd,
> Unruffled, like high Gods, ye liv'd and ruled:
> Now I behold in you fear, hope, and wrath;
> Actions of rage and passion; even as
> I see them, on the mortal world beneath,
> In men who die.—This is the grief, O Son!
> Sad sign of ruin, sudden dismay, and fall![25]

Coelus, who belongs to the old order and does not understand the situation, exhorts Hyperion, the one unconquered Titan, to use force. Later we see Saturn himself,

[24] *Hyperion*, ii. 335 ff.

[25] *Ibid.*, i. 329 ff. Cf. Sandys (ed. 1640, p. 15): "The Giants were the sonnes of the Earth (for so they called of old the ignorant, and earthly minded: as those the sonnes of heaven, who were admired for their vertues) said to be of a huge proportion; in that commonly such are prone to intemperance, wrath, and injustice; seldome yeelding unto reason, but are carried with the swinge of their lusts and affections." Like many poets before him, Keats confuses Giants and Titans (De Selincourt, pp. 486, 505-06).

the supreme God
At war with all the frailty of grief,
Of rage, of fear, anxiety, revenge,
Remorse, spleen, hope, but most of all despair.

Thus, even though the Titans were

symbols divine,
Manifestations of that beauteous life
Diffus'd unseen throughout eternal space,

they failed to justify the continuance of their reign. Hence the larger vision and wisdom of Oceanus, who alone among them has "wandered to eternal truth," and who now is able to envisage circumstance, all calm. He alone, except weak Clymene, whose glimpse of truth is only sensuous and emotional, can see the glow of superior beauty in the eyes of his successor and acknowledge the rightness of defeat.

When Apollo passes from aching ignorance to knowledge, the god, the true poet, is born.

Knowledge enormous makes a God of me.
Names, deeds, gray legends, dire events, rebellions,
Majesties, sovran voices, agonies,
Creations and destroyings, all at once
Pour into the wide hollows of my brain,
And deify me, as if some blithe wine
Or bright elixir peerless I had drunk,
And so become immortal.

The most important passage in the first book of *Endymion*—the answer to the question "Wherein lies happiness?"—contained a similar list of symbols of human history, but there the emphasis was on the clear religion of heaven, the "oneness" enjoyed by the soul that felt a bond with nature and legend, and that oneness was the first stage of experience leading to friendship and love. The lines in *Hyperion* have less of nature and of self, and more of the rise and fall of nations, the whole chaotic story of man's troubled past. Keats is not here concerned with the source of happiness, or with love, but with the knowledge that is sorrow, the sorrow that is wisdom. And the bright elixir that Apollo has drunk is no opiate that carries him Lethewards, away from the fever and fret of the world of man, for Keats has attained, potentially, his poetic manhood. "Was there a Poet born?" he had asked in *I Stood Tip-toe,* as he thought, wtih a charming mythological fancy, of the marriage night of Diana and Endymion. The poetic birth of Apollo takes place on the farther side of the vale of soul-making.

In addition to the reasons already indicated for the abandonment of *Hyperion,* Keats may have had one of his revulsions against a too high and hard conception of poetry. At any rate he wrote *The Eve of St. Agnes* and the odes; late in the summer he wrote *Lamia,* and set about the recasting of *Hyperion. The Fall of Hyperion* was his last effort to integrate his faculties and impulses, and to set forth his conception of the poet and the poet's function in the world. In *Hyperion* the meaning of Apollo's spiritual birth-pangs had been left somewhat obscure; the objective manner of presentation was not natural to one who had always written directly out of his own feelings, and perhaps he did not quite know what to do with the god when he had got him. The narrative in the *Fall* seems to carry out the general intention of *Hyperion,* but, by the late summer of 1819, Keats's failing health, the prolonged fever of his love for Fanny Brawne, pecuniary troubles, perhaps most of all the conviction that the topmost heights of poetry were not to be won by a divided soul, such causes as these had deepened and embittered his despair over himself, his past and his future.[26] In the symbolism of the garden, the temple, and the shrine, we have perhaps another variation on the three Wordsworthian stages of development, from sensuous pleasure to humanitarian concern for the world. But the sketch of poetic evolution is not now, as in *Sleep and Poetry,* partly wishful prophecy. Keats is here looking back on what seem to him to be the facts of his brief career, and he condemns himself, with harsh sincerity, for having dwelt in an ivory tower, for having given to men the illusive balm of dreams, whereas true poets, by intense effort, seize upon the reality which is not illusive. To them, as to active benefactors of humanity, the miseries of the world are misery, and will not let them rest.[27]

[26] On November 19 we have a gloomy letter to George, who needs money; Mr. Abbey wants John "to turn Bookseller"; he has tried to write lately but cannot get on while George is in such low water. Looking back over his *annus mirabilis,* he can say: "Nothing could have in all its circumstances fallen out worse for me than the last year has done, or could be more damping to my poetical talent—I comfort myself in the idea that you are a consolation to each other" (*Letters,* pp. 442-43).

[27] These lines seem to embody a recollection of the preface to *Alastor,* as Bradley suggested (*Oxford Lectures on Poetry,* 1920, pp. 242-43). In connection with active benefactors of humanity, and poets, one may quote from a letter written at this time: "I am convinced more and more day by day that fine writing is next to fine doing, the top thing in the world, the Paradise Lost becomes a greater wonder" (*Letters,* p. 374; August 24, 1819).

One need not be a sentimentalist to feel the profound personal tragedy not only in the self-laceration of this last effort to feel the giant agony of the world, but also in Keats's turning aside from the *Fall* to enjoy a last serene "sensation" in *To Autumn*. We do not endorse his condemnation of a large part of his work, but we can understand his attitude, can even see that the whole course of his development made it inevitable. As he said himself, the genius of poetry must work out its own salvation in a man, and we cannot guess, if he had had health and some measure of contentment, what would have been his ultimate solution and achievement. His house was, most of the time, divided against itself, but his consciousness of the fissure, his unceasing endeavor to solve the problem of sense and knowledge, art and humanity, are in themselves an index of his stature. No other English poet of the century had his poetic endowment, and no other strove so intensely to harmonize what may, without undue stretching of the terms, be called the Apollonian and the Faustian ideals of poetry. However high one's estimate of what he wrote, one may really think—to use an often meaningless cliché—that Keats was greater than his poems.

Synaesthetic Imagery in Keats

by Richard H. Fogle

Synaesthesia in Keats is a natural concomitant of other qualities of his poetry. Keats's verse is extraordinarily rich in sense-images, and his sense-imagery is very full and comprehensive.[1] He has at his command an unexampled abundance of vivid sensory images. Therefore he slips readily from one order of sensation to another when it suits his poetic purpose, like a master improviser who transposes his theme into a different key. Strong sensation is thus made to reinforce weak by his unusually powerful faculty of association; an odor-image may in a flash of associational intuition be transformed into an image of weight, or a sound-image take on the added sense of touch. Furthermore, synaesthesia is unusually fusional and swift in action, and Keats's poetry is fusional and compact in the highest degree, the more so as it gains in maturity. The "intensity" of his verse is a result of intense compression, like a molten ore sublimed by enormous pressures.[2]

The synaesthetic imagery of Keats is almost always actuated by a desire to attain the fullest possible sensuous effect. It frequently appears as a tendency to ally sense-images with the sense of touch in order to make them stronger and more concrete.[3] Whatever combination of sensations

[1] "The imagery of Keats's poetry has two notable characteristics. In the first place, it is comprehensive, having images of all the sensations of the sensory system—sensations of sight, hearing, touch, temperature, pressure, taste, smell, motor sensations, hunger, thirst, lust, etc. In the second place, it is sensuous, being rich in images of the intimately physical sensations of touch, temperature, pressure, taste, smell, and the internal sensations."—Claude Lee Finney, *The Evolution of Keats's Poetry*, II, 548.

[2] M. R. Ridley has recorded in his *Keats' Craftsmanship* the history of the poet's constant effort to attain the greatest possible compression and force in expressions. See also W. J. Bate, *Negative Capability,* pp. 53 ff., on the relationship between Keats' tendency toward intense condensation and his "fusion of the senses."

[3] *Ibid.,* p. 54.

he may happen to employ, however, he invariably invokes a stronger sense to reinforce a comparatively weak one.

Keats's pursuit of rich, full, sensuous effects is incidental to a more arduous quest, his search for fullness and completeness of meaning. Sensation, powerful though it is in Keats's poetry, is but a single element in a highly complex unity. Consequently his fusions and transferences of sensation are incidental to his deeper, more complex syntheses of poetic experience, in which intellect, sense, and emotion are inseparably interwoven. His synaesthetic imagery is an outward manifestation of his intuitive sense of the Oneness of things, of the relationships between widely separate and dissimilar phenomena, of the intimate kinship of man and nature. The secret of many of his sense-analogies lies in his unrivalled ability to absorb, sympathize with, and humanize natural objects, with effortless and instinctive ease. . . .

Synaesthesia in the poetry of Keats is generally compressive, complexly associational, functional, and unobtrusive. His sense-analogies are for the most part prepared for and explained by their contexts. In one of his not infrequent references to wine, for example, pleasure in its chill is synaesthetically allied to delight in its rich coloring:

> . . . Here is wine,
> Alive with sparkles—never, I aver,
> Since Ariadne was a vintager,
> So *cool a purple* . . .
>
> (*Endymion,* II, 441-44)

"Cool" is a quality of "purple," but "purple" is in part merely a metaphor for "wine," so that the figure balances precariously, ready to slip in two different directions. This relationship of "cool-wine" as well as "cool-purple" lends to the image a common-sense verisimilitude which renders it easily acceptable, and lessens the surprise of the fusion of visual and tactual sensations. The synaesthetic effect results in some degree from intensely compressed expression.

Similarly complex are Endymion's impressions of water-spray in his journey through the underworld. The spray rises before him "Alive, and *dazzling cool* . . ." (II, 608-9). The visual and tactual sensations of "dazzling" and "cool" are simultaneous, but they do not fuse, since they are to be referred not to each other but to Endymion who experiences them. Compression is once more the principal synaesthetic agent. Yet another example occurs in *Isabella:*

Soon she turn'd up a soiled glove, whereon
Her silk had play'd in *purple* phantasies . . .

(ll. 369-70)

Common sense may be easily satisfied by the reflection that "purple" is doubtless the color of the silk. But "purple" is also the sensuous contact of the lovers' gloved hands, and the emotion aroused by this contact. It is a sensuous-imaginative symbol of the warm, instinctive young love of Isabella and Lorenzo,[4] and epitomizes the whole generous, sensual, sentimental tone of a poem which Keats stigmatized as "too smokeable," "weak-sided," and afflicted with "an amusing sober-sadness." [5]

Of a like complexity is this startling synaesthetic image from *Endymion:*

. . . lost in pleasure at her feet he sinks,
Touching with *dazzled lips her starlight hand.*

(*Endymion,* IV, 418-19)

The interplay of sight and touch is very swift.[6] There is a trace of "wit," of conscious ingenuity, which lends to the image a certain flavour of modernity. The lips of Endymion are "dazzled," of course, because the hand which they touch is "starlight." But there is more to the image than its sensory content. Endymion is dazzled because he is dreaming that he is among the Gods on Olympus, kneeling before Hebe: a situation in which some bedazzlement seems excusable. The Immortals may reasonably be presumed to be possessed of "brightness," traditionally an attribute of Godhead. Even as Endymion dreams, he is floating high above the earth on the back of a supernatural steed, amid a dusk sky in which the first stars of evening and the moon are about to appear. Endymion is in love with the Moon-Goddess, and he is the hero of a poem saturated with references to moonlight. The image in question is on the surface a witty

[4] Purple synaesthetically used as a emblem of youthful, passionate love occurs also in *The Eve of St. Agnes:*

Sudden a thought came like a full-blown rose,
Flushing his cheek, and in his pained heart
Made *purple* riot . . . (ll. 136-38).

Here "purple" has emotional associations with "thought—full-blown rose," and physical suggestions of the idea of "hearts blood."

[5] *The Letters of John Keats,* Oxford (1935), p. 391.

[6] Miss June E. Downey has cited this image as a probable case of "true" synaesthesia, reflecting a genuine sense-idiosyncrasy in Keats.—"Literary Synesthesia," *op. cit.,* p. 497. I am inclined to doubt this; the peculiarities of the figure can be adequately accounted for in terms of purely literary considerations

conceit, with undertones of meaning and tendrils of association attaching it on every side to its context, adding contrapuntal emotional and romantic strains which soften its initial hardness.

Much of Keats's most characteristic synaesthetic imagery reinforces sound or odor with strong tactual, organic, or kinesthetic sensations. In *Endymion,*

> . . . we might
> Be *incense-pillowed* every summer night
>
> (II, 998-99)

gives body, weight, and softness to an olfactory image. As is so frequently the case in Keats, the expression is complex and compressive. One may read the lines as "we might lie every summer night on clouds of incense so thick that they seem to have weight, and can even support our bodies"; and more matter-of-factly, "we might lie on pillows impregnated with incense." The overripe lusciousness which this image shares with so much of *Endymion* causes it to suffer by comparison with the very similar image "what soft incense hangs upon the boughs," in the *Ode to a Nightingale,* in which the implications of "soft" and "hangs" become plain only on careful scrutiny. These images of touch and weight function quietly and organically as single threads in the rich, heavy fabric of the verse. Likewise quiet and unobtrusive is the synaesthetic mingling of touch, temperature, odor, and sight in the description of Hyperion's palace-door, which is

> . . . like a rose in vermeil tint and shape,
> In fragrance *soft,* and *coolness* to the eye.
>
> (*Hyperion,* I, 209-10)

"Fragrance" is more vividly realized by virtue of the image of touch which accompanies it. "Coolness to the eye," although instantaneous in effect, proposes a sense-relationship familiar to most of us, and generally accepted as normal.

On one occasion Keats speaks of the coolness of light itself:

> He turned—there was a whelming sound—he stept,
> There was a *cooler* light . . .
>
> (*Endymion,* II, 1018-19)

This close-knit combination of tactual and visual is fusional and intense. The poet is trying to describe in a single adjective the essential differentiating quality of the light, and he has found it necessary to resort to a different order of sensation. The image can also be explained naturalistically. The "whelming sound" and altered light is of the sea, which has but now swept over Endymion's head. "Cooler" can in part be referred to the feel of the water on his body, and to the fact that the sun's rays must obviously have less force when they are filtered through the sea above him. As in other instances, the image merges within itself a complex set of associations latent in its context.

There is a striking mixture of visual pleasure and tactual feeling at the beginning of *Hyperion,* Bk. III, as Keats invokes the delights of earth to welcome Apollo to his yet unconquered realm:

> Let the rose *glow* intense and *warm* in the air.
>
> (l. 15)

The image seems primarily verbal in origin, however. The notion of a *glowing* rose is not surprising. Keats appears to have used "glow" metaphorically, without considering its sensory properties, and to have been led by the tactual quality inherent in it to the more forthright and daring "warm."

Keats comes closest to the individuality of feeling and suddenness of effect which characterizes modern synaesthesia in an image which attributes color to organic feeling:

> The colours all inflamed throughout her train,
> She writh'd about, convuls'd with *scarlet pain.*
>
> (*Lamia,* I, 153-54)

"Scarlet" is undoubtedly an attribute of "pain," in a surprising and instantaneous sense-transference. As usual, however, the context provides a further explanation. The snake Lamia has herself turned scarlet in the process of her transformation into a woman, and the change naturally involves a good deal of suffering. Consequently there remains an ambiguity of meaning, resulting from the intense condensation of Keats's expression. "Scarlet" and "pain" on the one hand fuse with each other; on the other they are merely parallel and co-temporal.

Keats describes sound even more sensuously than light and odor, by the same device of reinforcing the weaker sense with a stronger: most frequently tactual, sometimes organic or kinesthetic, sometimes two or more different senses in conjunction. In his poetry sound and music are often tangible and material, with weight, texture and form.[7] In the banquet-room passage in *Lamia* music is possessed of architectural solidity and strength:

> A haunting music, sole perhaps and lone
> Supportress of the faery roof, made moan
> Throughout, as fearful the whole charm might fade.
>
> (II, 122-24)

Sound is sometimes silver or golden. The image

> . . . other harmonies, stopped short
> Leave the dinn'd air vibrating *silverly,*
>
> (*Hyperion,* II, 127-28)

is the most definitely synaesthetic among Keats's figures of this sort, because it is most compact and unequivocal. The poet somehow manages to convey the impression that the unusual "silverly" is the only possible word for the occasion; there is, as it were, a matter-of-factness and calm certainty in his use of it. The music of the Bacchic revellers in *Endymion*—

> The earnest trumpet spake, and *silver* thrills
> From kissing cymbals made a merry din
>
> (IV, 197-98)

is closely analogous, but one cannot take "silver" so seriously and literally as the "silverly" of the previous passage. It is more closely connected with the idea of sound-vibration, and less nearly autonomous. "Golden," in

> And scarce three steps, ere Music's golden tongue
> Flattered to tears this aged man and poor
>
> (*The Eve of St. Agnes,* ll. 20-21)

has a significance almost entirely emotional; it is not visible or material. "Silver, snarling trumpets" (*The Eve of St. Agnes,* l. 31) is ambiguous. Silver is naturalistically and prosaically the substance of the trumpets, and it is also the quality of their tone.

Sound in Keats's poetry often has texture. Whether it is the music of man or nature, it is generally soft and smooth, seldom harsh. The wind, for example,

[7] Cf. Downey, "Literary Synesthesia," *op. cit.,* p. 495.

. . . that now did stir
About the crisped oaks full drearily,
Yet with as sweet a softness as might be
Remembered from its *velvet summer song*
(*Endymion,* IV, 294-97)

is heavy, tangible, and soft. There is much the same effect in

. . . his palace-door flew ope
In *smoothest silence,* save what solemn tubes,
(*Hyperion,* I, 205-6)

but "smoothest" is fusional and complex. It is an attribute of "silence," of the movement of the doors, and by a transfer associational in origin, of "solemn tubes."

Taste-images occur with relative infrequency in Keats's synaesthetic imagery, but such as appear are powerful and vivid. On one occasion he combines taste with smell to produce one of the strongest of all his sensory images:

Also, when he would taste the spicy wreaths
Of incense, breath'd aloft from sacred hills,
Instead of sweets, his ample palate took
Savour of poisonous brass and metal sick . . .
(*Hyperion,* I, 186-89)

The gustatory and the olfactory are thoroughly mingled, the stronger taste reinforcing the less immediate olfactory sensation. The whole has a massive solidity, from the concentration of effects in *taste, spicy, incense, breath'd, sweets, palate, savour,* and *poisonous;* to which are added suggestions of weight and solidity in *ample, brass,* and *metal. Sick* rounds off the passage with an organic image.

A complex but perfect and as it were unconscious fusion binds together taste, sound, and sight in the lines from *Isabella*

. . . O turn thee to the very tale,
And *taste* the *music* of that *vision* pale.
(*Isabella,* ll.391-92)

As was suggested in the previous chapter, it sometimes appears that the primary source of Keats's inspiration lies in his senses. He begins with the feel, or in this particular instance with the taste, of the poem. Three orders of sensation are here welded together with such ease and apparent inevitability that there is little feeling of jar or paradox. Keats is talking of his original in Boccaccio, and to his perceptions the "music" of the prose, the "taste" of it, and the visual images aroused by it are identical. Another example of the poet's ability to *feel* himself into a situation is "In *pale* and *silver* silence they remain'd . . ." (*Hyperion,* II, 356). The Titans, at sombre council in a rocky valley, are aroused by the first faint gleam of the rising sun as their brother Hyperion comes slowly into view over a distant peak. "Pale" and "silver" characterize "silence"; they describe the light now filtering down; they symbolize the mood of the fallen deities; and they cast a solemnity over the whole scene, harmonizing nature with the quiet despair of its late rulers. These images are highly functional, fusional, and compressive. They epitomize much in little space.

The easy naturalness and functional quality characteristic of the synaesthetic imagery of Keats is especially notable in his later poetry, more particularly in the six great odes. In the odes divergent sensations and notions are fused into complex but indivisible wholes by the intense concentration of his mature technique. His sense-analogies work quietly, in the main almost unnoticed, but they are effectual in aiding to produce the rich and sensuous atmosphere of his most finished poetry. The *Ode to Psyche* presents a remarkable instance of fusion and transference of multiple sensations, so quietly managed that the variety and diversity of the materials is likely to be overlooked:

> Mid *hush'd,* cool-rooted flowers, *fragrant-eyed,*
> Blue, silver-white, and budded Tyrian . . .
>
> (ll. 13-14)

Auditory, tactual, olfactory, and visual suggestions join together in one line in perfect amity, to be transformed by a synthesizing and compressive process into a unity different from any of these and yet comprising all.

In the *Ode to a Nightingale* two single images and the famous "blushful Hippocrene" passage exemplify the typical qualities of Keatsian synaesthesia.

> In some *melodious* plot
> Of beechen green . . .
>
> (ll. 8-9)

and

> . . . here there is no light
> Save what from heaven is with the breezes *blown*
>
> (ll. 38-39)

are "inevitable"; they are fully and immediately acceptable in their quiet rightness. In the first the idea of the bird is transferred to, and fuses with the locale. The song of the nightingale merges with the foliage of the soft spring night in a single impression. In the second image one overlooks the unusual sense-transference of light blown with the breezes because it is at once obvious that Keats has consummately described the effect of glancing light filtering down through leaves stirred gently by the wind.

The synaesthetic imagery of Keats reaches its highest level, however, in the complex fusion of sense, emotion, and concept of the second stanza of the Nightingale:

> O, for a draught of vintage! that hath been
> Cool'd a long age in the deep-delved earth,
> *Tasting* of Flora and the country green,
> Dance, and Provençal song, and *sunburnt* mirth!
> O for a *beaker* full of the *warm South,*
> Full of the true, the blushful Hippocrene,
> With beaded bubbles winking at the brim,
> And purple-stained mouth . . .

Keats has attained to the utmost degree of synthesizing compression in this passage, packing into a few lines what prose could not have expressed in many times the number of words he has employed. As in the figure from *Isabella,* "*taste* the music of that vision pale," he begins sensuously with the *taste* of his experience. The imagined contact of the wine with his palate evokes through a complex associational process a series of pictures and feelings, very much as in Proust's *Swann's Way* the savour of a cup of tea draws up the emotional and pictorial drama of the past from the depths of the subconscious, where it has long lain buried.[8] The associations of the wine at first seem somewhat arbitrary. The relation between *Flora* and the *country green* is obvious enough: the thought of the Goddess of Flowers naturally calls up ideas of the fertile, peaceful green-

[8] *Swann's Way,* in *Remembrance of Things Past,* tr. C. K. Scott Moncrieff, I, 54-241. Proust, of course, recalls his own past experience, while Keats's images are complex products of his imagination.

ness of a rural scene. Yet "Dance, and Provençal song, and sunburnt mirth" are further to seek. Each new image joins harmoniously with its predecessor, but if we stop to examine we observe that this is an imaginative, not a logical unity; to discern the agents of this synthesis one must put forth effort. *Country green* easily shifts into *country dance, dance* suggests its accompanying *song,* and *country, dance,* and *song* combine to produce the compressed synaesthetic fusion of *sunburnt mirth,* which when unfolded for examination discloses a merry festival of country folk, bronzed by their labors beneath the summer sun. *Dance* we may likewise relate to Flora through the flower-bedecked dance of goddesses in Botticelli's "Primavera." *Provençal* is generally associated, aside from the fame of Provence in song, with ideas of gaiety. It looks backward also to "Cool'd a long age in the deep-delved earth," for the associations of the wine are with the Romantic past, at one moment with some dim mythological Golden Age of Flora, the next with the days of troubadours and the *gai science* of Provençal poetry.

The image *tasting* is thus synaesthetically fused not only with other sensations, but with concept and emotion as well in a single imaginative whole. The surprising figures,

> With beaded bubbles winking at the brim,
> And purple-stained mouth,

are synaesthetic through quick shifts of sensation, tactual, visual, and gustatory; but the effect of synaesthesia comes principally from half-hidden but powerful personifications. As in earlier instances, the elements of these analogies are referable not to each other, but to an underlying agent of organization. Here, the beaker is a bleary Silenus, with *winking,* drunken eyes, and *purple-stained mouth.*

Negative Capability

by Walter Jackson Bate

I

The "Negative Capability" letter is best understood as another phrasing of these thoughts, with at least three further extensions. First, the problem of form or style in art enters more specifically. Second, the ideal toward which he is groping is contrasted more strongly with the egoistic assertion of one's own identity. Third, the door is further opened to the perception—which he was to develop within the next few months—of the sympathetic potentialities of the imagination.

He begins by telling his brothers that he has gone to see Edmund Kean, has written his review, and is enclosing it for them. Then on Saturday, December 20, he went to see an exhibition of the American painter, Benjamin West, particularly his picture, "Death on the Pale Horse." Keats was altogether receptive to any effort to attain the "sublime," and West's painting had been praised for succeeding. Yet is struck Keats as flat—"there is nothing to be intense upon; no women one feels mad to kiss; no face swelling into reality." Then the first crucial statement appears:

> The excellence of every Art is its intensity, capable of making all disagreeables evaporate, from their being in close relationship with Beauty & Truth—Examine King Lear & you will find this exemplified throughout; but in this picture we have unpleasantness without any momentous depth of speculation excited, in which to bury its repulsiveness.

In the active cooperation or full "greeting" of the experiencing imagination and its object, the nature or "identity" of the object is grasped so vividly that only those associations and qualities that are strictly relevant to the central conception remain. The irrelevant and discordant (the "disagreeables") "evaporate" from this fusion of object and mind. Hence "Truth" and "Beauty" spring simultaneously into being, and also begin to approximate each other. For, on the one hand, the external reality—otherwise overlooked, or at most only sleepily acknowledged, or dissected so that a particular aspect of it may be abstracted for special purposes of argument or thought—has now, as it were, awakened into "Truth": it has been met by that human recognition, fulfilled and extended by that human agreement with reality, which we call "truth." And at the same time, with the irrelevant "evaporated," this dawning into unity is felt as "Beauty." Nor is it a unity solely of the object itself, emerging untrammeled and in its full significance, but a unity also of the human spirit, both within itself and with what was at first outside it. For in this "intensity"—the "excellence," he now feels, "of every Art"—we attain, if only for a while, a harmony of the inner life with truth. It is in this harmony that "Beauty" and "Truth" come together. The "pleasant," in the ordinary sense of the word, has nothing to do with the point being discussed; and to introduce it is only to trivialize the conception of "Beauty." Hence Keats's reference to *Lear*. The reality disclosed may be distressing and even cruel to human nature. But the harmony with truth will remain, and even deepen, to the extent that the emerging reality is being constantly matched at every stage by the "depth of speculation excited"—by the corresponding release and extension, in other words, of human insight. "Examine King Lear and you will find this exemplified throughout."

Hazlitt's short essay "On Gusto" had aroused his thinking about style when he read it at Oxford in the *Round Table;* and what he is saying now is partly the result of what he has assimilated from Hazlitt.[1] By "gusto," Hazlitt means an excitement of the imagination in which the perceptive identification with the object is almost complete, and the living character of the object is caught and shared in its full diversity and given vital expression in art. It is "power or passion defining any object." But the result need not be subjective. By grasping sympathetically the overall significance of the object, the "power or passion" is able to cooperate, so to speak, with that significance—to go the full distance with its potentialities, omitting the irrelevant (which Keats calls the "disagreeables"), and conceiving the object with its various qualities coalescing

[1] Keats had also read Hazlitt's own essay on Benjamin West in the December issue of the *Edinburgh Review* (*Works,* XVIII [1933], 135-140), where West is censored for lack of "gusto."

into the vital unity that is the object itself. One result is that the attributes or qualities that we glean through our different senses of sight, hearing, touch, and the rest are not presented separately or piecemeal, but "the impression made on one sense excites by affinity those of another." Thus Claude Lorrain's landscapes, though "perfect abstractions of the visible images of things," lack "gusto": "They do not interpret one sense by another . . . That is, his eye wanted imagination; it did not strongly sympathise with his other faculties. He saw the atmosphere, but he did not feel it." Chaucer's descriptions of natural scenery have gusto: they give "the very feeling of the air, the coolness or moisture of the ground." "There is gusto in the colouring of Titian. Not only do his heads seem to think—his bodies seem to feel."

II

This interplay and coalescence of impressions was to become a conscious aim in Keats's own poetry within the next six months, and, by the following autumn, to be fulfilled as richly as by any English poet of the last three centuries. Meanwhile, only a few days before he wrote the "Negative Capability" letter to his brothers, he had followed Hazlitt's use of the word "gusto" in his own review "On Edmund Kean as a Shakespearian Actor" (though he later returns to the word "intensity"—"gusto" perhaps suggesting a briskness or bounce of spirit he does not have in mind). He had been trying in this review to describe how "a melodious passage in poetry" may attain a fusion of "both sensual and spiritual," where each extends and declares itself by means of the other:

> The spiritual is felt when the very letters and points of charactered language show like the hieroglyphics of beauty;—the mysterious signs of an immortal free-masonry! . . . To one learned in Shakespearian hieroglyphics, —learned in the spiritual portion of those lines to which Kean adds a sensual grandeur: his tongue must seem to have robbed "the Hybla bees, and left them honeyless."

Hence "there is an indescribable gusto in his voice, by which we feel that the utterer is thinking of the past and future, while speaking of the present." [2]

Keats is here extending the notion of "gusto" in a way that applies prophetically to his own maturer style—to an imaginative "intensity" of conception, that is, in which process, though slowed to an insistent pres-

[2] Hampstead Keats, V.229-230.

ent, is carried in active solution. So with the lines he had quoted a month before to Reynolds as an example of Shakespeare's "intensity of working out conceits":

> When lofty trees I see barren of leaves
> Which erst from heat did canopy the herd,
> And Summer's green all girded up in sheaves,
> Borne on the bier with white and bristly beard.

Previous functions, and the mere fact of loss itself, are a part of the truth of a thing as it now is. The nature of the "lofty trees" in this season, now "barren of leaves," includes the fact that they formerly "from heat did canopy the herd"; nor is it only the dry, completed gain of the autumn that is "girded up in sheaves," but the "Summer's green" that it once was. This entire way of thinking about style is proving congenial to Keats in the highest degree; for though it has independent developments, it has also touched and is giving content to the ideal briefly suggested a year before in *Sleep and Poetry*—even before he saw the Elgin Marbles for the first time: an ideal of poetry as "might half slumb'ring on its own right arm." The delight in energy caught in momentary repose goes back to the idea he had "when a Schoolboy . . . of an heroic painting": "I saw it somewhat sideways," he tells Haydon, "large prominent round and colour'd with magnificence—somewhat like the feel I have of Anthony and Cleopatra. Or of Alcibiades, leaning on his Crimson Couch in his Galley, his broad shoulders imperceptibly heaving with the Sea." So with the line in *Henry VI,* "See how the surly Warwick mans the Wall." One of the comments he wrote in his copy of Milton during the next year gives another illustration:

> Milton in every instance pursues his imagination to the utmost—he is "sagacious of his Quarry," he sees Beauty on the wing, pounces upon it and gorges it to the producing his essential verse. . . . But in no instance is this sort of perseverance more exemplified than in what may be called his *stationing or statu[a]ry.* He is not content with simple description, he must station,—thus here, we not only see how the Birds *"with clang despised the ground,"* but we see them *"under a cloud in prospect."* So we see Adam *"Fair indeed and tall—under a plantane"*—and so we see Satan *"disfigured—on the Assyrian Mount."* [3]

[3] Hampstead Keats, V.303-304. The comment is written next to the passage in *Paradise Lost,* VI.420-423:

> but feather'd soon and fledge
> They summ'd their pens, and, soaring the air sublime,
> With clang despised the ground, under a cloud
> In prospect.

The union of the ideal of dynamic poise, of power kept in reserve, with the ideal of range of implication suggests one principal development in his own style throughout the next year and a half. The very triumph of this union—as triumphs often tend to do—could have proved an embarrassment to later ideals and interests had it become an exclusive stylistic aim. However magnificent the result in the great odes, in portions of *Hyperion,* or in what Keats called the "colouring" and "drapery" of *The Eve of St. Agnes,* it carried liabilities in both pace and variety that would have to be circumvented for successful narrative and, above all, dramatic poetry. But even at the moment, and throughout the next year, what he calls "intensity"—the "greeting of the Spirit" and its object—is by no means completely wedded to a massive centering of image through poise and "stationing." If his instinctive delight in fullness was strengthened in one direction by the Elgin Marbles— which he still made visits to see—other, more varied appeals to his ready empathy were being opened and reinforced by his reading of Shakespeare.

III

The second and longer of the crucial parts of the "Negative Capability" letter is preceded by some more remarks about what he has been doing since his brothers left, and the remarks provide a significant preface. He had dinner—"I have been out too much lately"—with "Horace Smith & met his two Brothers with [Thomas] Hill & [John] Kingston & one [Edward] Du Bois."

Partly because he himself was so direct and—as Bailey said—"transparent," he was ordinarily tolerant of the more innocent affectations by which people hope to establish superiority. Moreover, such affectations appealed to his enormous relish for the idiosyncratic. As the next year passed, the very futility of such brief postures—the pointless intricacy of these doomed stratagems—against the vast backdrop of a universe of constantly unfolding "uncertainties, Mysteries, doubts," was also to take on a pathos for him. . . .

So at Horace Smith's dinner, which he describes to George and Tom, where he met five other men of literary interests. Their entire way of talking about literature fatigued him for the moment. The possible uses of literature seemed frozen into posture, into mannerism. Given his attempts to approach his new ideal of "disinterestedness," and the thoughts of "Humility" and of openness to amplitude that had become more specific, even more convinced, within the last few months, the gathering typified the exact opposite of what was wanted:

> They only served to convince me, how superior humour is to wit in respect to enjoyment—These men say things which make one start, without making one feel, they are all alike; their manners are alike; they all know fashionable; they have a mannerism in their very eating & drinking, in their mere handling a Decanter—They talked of Kean & his low company—Would I were with that company instead of yours said I to myself! I know such like acquaintance will never do for me.

But his humor was to return when he found himself again in Kingston's company at Haydon's a week and a half afterwards. The "mannerism" in the "mere handling a Decanter" had caught his fancy as a symbol of the entire evening. At Haydon's, as he gleefully told George and Tom, "I astonished Kingston at supper . . . keeping my two glasses at work in a knowing way."

Shortly after Smith's literary party, he went to the Christmas pantomime at Drury Lane with Charles Brown and Charles Dilke. Walking with them back to Hampstead, he found himself having

> not a dispute but a disquisition with Dilke, on various subjects; several things dovetailed in my mind, & at once it struck me, what quality went to form a Man of Achievement especially in Literature & which Shakespeare possessed so enormously—I mean *Negative Capability,* that is when man is capable of being in uncertainties, Mysteries, doubts, without any irritable reaching after fact & reason—Coleridge, for instance, would let go by a fine isolated verisimilitude caught from the Penetralium of mystery, from being incapable of remaining content with half knowledge. This pursued through Volumes would perhaps take us no further than this, that with a great poet the sense of Beauty overcomes every other consideration, or rather obliterates all consideration.

Using what we know of the background, we could paraphrase these famous sentences as follows. In our life of uncertainties, where no one system or formula can explain everything—where even a word is at best, in Bacon's phrase, a "wager of thought"—what is needed is an imaginative openness of mind and heightened receptivity to reality in its full and diverse concreteness. This, however, involves negating one's own ego. Keats's friend Dilke, as he said later, "was a Man who cannot feel he has a personal identity unless he has made up his Mind about every thing. The only means of strengthening one's intellect is to make up one's mind about nothing—to let the mind be a thoroughfare for all thoughts. . . .

Dilke will never come at a truth as long as he lives; because he is always trying at it." To be dissatisfied with such insights as one may attain through this openness, to reject them unless they can be wrenched into a part of a systematic structure of one's own making, is an egoistic assertion of one's own identity. The remark, "without any irritable reaching after fact and reason," is often cited as though the pejorative words are "fact and reason," and as though uncertainties were being preferred for their own sake. But the significant word, of course, is "irritable." We should also stress "capable"—"capable of being in uncertainties, Mysteries, doubts" without the "irritable" need to extend our identities and rationalize our "half knowledge." For a "great poet" especially, a sympathetic absorption in the essential significance of his object (caught and relished in that active cooperation of the mind in which the emerging "Truth" is felt as "Beauty," and in which the harmony of the human imagination and its object is attained) "overcomes every other consideration" (considerations that an "irritable reaching after fact and reason" might otherwise itch to pursue). Indeed, it goes beyond and "obliterates" the act of "consideration"—of deliberating, analyzing, and piecing experience together through "consequitive reasoning."

IV

Such speculations could hardly be called more than a beginning. Taken by themselves they could lead almost anywhere. That, of course, was one of their principal assets. Even so, the need for at least some specific and positive procedures, helpful at any period of life, is particularly pressing at twenty-two. Keats understandably wavered throughout the next few months in trying to interpret whatever premises he had attained thus far —premises that were hardly more than the penumbra of the idea of "disinterestedness" as it touched his concrete experience. Such shadows at least involved extensions of a sort; and the thought of this was to give him some consolation as time passed.

But meanwhile he had moments when something close to mere passivity appealed strongly; and the image of the receptive flower, visited and fertilized by the bee, caught his fancy. The relentless labor of writing *Endymion* was producing a natural reaction. Insights, reconsiderations, "speculations" (to use his own word) overlooked during that huge scurry, were now presenting themselves more abundantly than ever before. Because the gains in having written the poem were becoming assimilated, they were at times almost forgotten. Slow development, maturity, rooted strength, leisure for growth, took on a further attraction. But in the very act of urging eloquently—and justly—the virtues of something not far from Wordsworth's "wise passiveness" the limitations would suddenly disclose themselves to him. He would begin to feel that this was not what he meant, or wanted, at all. At least it was not enough by itself. A letter to John Reynolds (February 19) finely illustrates the course of one "speculation." He starts with a now-favorite thought of his that any one point may serve as a fruitful beginning. A man could "pass a very pleasant life" if he sat down each day and

> read a certain Page of full Poesy or distilled Prose and let him wander with it, and muse upon it, and reflect from it and bring home to it, and prophesy upon it, and dream upon it—untill it becomes stale—but when will it do so? Never—When Man has arrived at a certain ripeness in intellect any one grand and spiritual passage serves him as a starting post towards all "the two-and-thirty Pallaces."

The result would be a genuine "voyage of conception." A doze on the sofa, a child's prattle, a strain of music, even "a nap upon Clover," could all engender "ethereal finger-pointings." It would have the impetus, the strength, of being self-directive. "Many have original Minds who do not think it—they are led away by Custom." The insight, substantiated by his own experience, leads him next to turn upside down the old fable of the spider and the bee, especially as Swift used it. The appeal of the spider as a symbol is that the points of leaves and twigs on which it begins its work can be very few, and yet it is able to fill the air with a "circuiting." "Now it appears to me that almost any Man may like the Spider spin from his own inwards his own airy Citadel," which will then be creatively meaningful—it will be "full of Symbols for his spiritual eye." Of course his starting-points, his "circuiting," and the achieved "space for his wandering," would all differ from that of others. If we wish to be militant, complications would result. Here Keats comes to the heart of his thought:

> The Minds of Mortals are so different and bent on such diverse Journeys that it may at first appear impossible for any common taste and fellowship to exist between two or three under these suppositions—It is however quite the contrary—Minds would leave each other in contrary directions, traverse each other in Numberless points, and all [at] last greet each other at the Journey's end—An old Man and a child would talk together and the old Man be led on his Path, and the child left thinking—Man should not dispute or assert but whisper results to his neighbour, and thus by every germ of Spirit

> sucking the Sap from mould ethereal every human might become great, and Humanity instead of being a wide heath of Furse and Briars with here and there a remote Oak or Pine, would become a grand democracy of Forest Trees.

At no later time would he have disagreed with what he has just said. But he carries the ideal of receptivity further in sentences that are sometimes separated from context and interpreted as a new, fundamental credo:

> It has been an old Comparison for our urging on—the Bee hive—however it seems to me that we should rather be the flower than the Bee . . . Now it is more noble to sit like Jove tha[n] to fly like Mercury—let us not therefore go hurrying about and collecting honey-bee like, buzzing here and there impatiently from a knowledge of what is to be arrived at: but let us open our leaves like a flower and be passive and receptive—budding patiently under the eye of Apollo and taking hints from every noble insect that favors us with a visit.

In this spirit he has just written the fine unrhymed sonnet, "What the Thrush Said," with its refrain "O fret not after knowledge." He had been "led into these thoughts . . . by the beauty of the morning operating on a sense of Idleness—I have not read any Books—the Morning said I was right—I had no Idea but of the Morning and the Thrush said I was right."

But as soon as he copies the poem for Reynolds, he becomes "sensible all this is a mere sophistication, however it may neighbour to any truths, to excuse my own indolence." There is not much chance of rivaling Jove anyway, and one can consider oneself "very well off as a sort of scullion-Mercury or even a humble Bee." Two days later he also tells his brothers that "The Thrushes are singing"; but he himself is now "reading Voltaire and Gibbon, although I wrote to Reynolds the other day to prove reading was of no use."

V

Wherever the more general implications might lead, he was clearer and more certain in his growing interest in the impersonality of genius, "especially in Literature." For here the ideal of "disinterestedness" directly touched an internal fund both of native gift and (considering his age) accumulated experience.

What strikes us most in his capacity for sympathetic identification, starting with the schooldays at Enfield, is its inclusiveness. This is not the volatile empathic range of even the rare actor. For the range is vertical as well as horizontal, and is distinguished more by an adhesive purchase of mind than by volubility. He might, in describing the bearbaiting to Clarke, instinctively begin to imitate not only the spectators but the bear, "dabbing his fore paws hither and thither," and, in diagnosing Clarke's stomach complaint and comparing the stomach to a brood of baby-birds "gaping for sustenance," automatically open his own "capacious mouth." But empathic expressions of this sort were mere side-effects—like the self-forgetful fights at Enfield—of an habitual capacity for identification that went deeper. When he picked up styles in the writing of poetry, it was not as a mimic or copyist but as a fellow participator identified even more with the other's aim and ideal than with the individual himself. If, when still a student at Guy's Hospital, he caught elements of Felton Mathew's style, he dignified them; and the result, poor as it is, transcends anything Mathew wrote. So later with Hunt. Except at the very start, and except for a few isolated passages afterwards, we have nothing of the routine mechanism of a copy. If anything, he brings Hunt more to life. Still later, in *Hyperion,* he was to write within little more than two or three months the only poem among all the Miltonic imitations in English that Milton himself might not have been ashamed to write.

Discussion of these larger manifestations would lead to a summary of his entire development as illustration. We can, however, linger for a moment on his delight in empathic imagery itself. For here, quickly and vividly, his ready sympathy appears long before anyone could have called his attention to such a thing or given him a vocabulary with which to describe it. We think back to Clarke's account of the lines and images that most caught Keats's imagination when they first read together at Enfield. Doubtless feeling the weight of the parting billows on his own shoulders, he "*hoisted* himself up, and looked burly and dominant, as he said, 'what an image that is—*sea-shouldering whales.*' " Much later there was the memorable introduction to Chapman's Homer, and the passage in the shipwreck of Ulysses that brought "one of his delighted stares": "Down he sank to death. / The sea had soak'd his heart through." His reading of Shakespeare, now that he was about to write with less sense of hurry, was beginning to encourage his gift for empathic concentration of image; and within two years this was to develop to a degree hardly rivaled since Shakespeare himself. Among the passages he excitedly copied out for Reynolds, a month before the "Negative Capability" letter, is the description of the trembling withdrawal of a snail into its shell:

He has left nothing to say about nothing or any thing: for look at Snails, you know what he says about Snails, you know where he talks about "cockled snails"—well . . . this is in the Venus and Adonis: the Simile brought it to my Mind.

> Audi—As the snail, whose tender horns being hit,
> Shrinks back into his shelly cave with pain,
> And there all smothered up in shade doth sit,
> Long after fearing to put forth again.[4]

So with the comment he later wrote in his copy of *Paradise Lost* (IX. 179-191):

> Satan having entered the Serpent, and inform'd his brutal sense—might seem sufficient—but Milton goes on *"but his sleep disturb'd not."* Whose spirit does not ache at the smothering and confinement—the unwilling stillness—the *"waiting close"*? Whose head is not dizzy at the possible speculations of satan in his serpent prison—no passage of poetry ever can give a greater pain of suffocation.[5]

Finally, before turning to the impact of Hazlitt, we may glance back a few months to Severn's account of his walks with Keats on Hampstead Heath during the preceding summer, while Keats was still working on Book II of *Endymion*. Nothing could bring him so quickly out of "one of his fits of seeming gloomful reverie" as his vivid identification with organic motion in what he called "the inland sea"—the movement of the wind across a field of grain. He "would stand, leaning forward," watching with a "serene look in his eyes and sometimes with a slight smile." At other times, "when 'a wave was billowing through a tree,' as he described the uplifting surge of air among swaying masses of chestnut or oak foliage," or when he would hear in the distance "the wind coming across woodlands,"

> "The tide! the tide!" he would cry delightedly, and spring on to some stile, or upon the low bough of a wayside tree, and watch the passage of the wind

[4] In a letter to Bailey written the same day is the often-quoted remark, "If a Sparrow come before my Window I take part in its existence and pick about the Gravel"—later echoed in the little poem, "Where's the Poet?":

> 'Tis the man who with a bird,
> Wren or eagle, finds his way to
> All its instincts; he hath heard
> The Lion's roaring, and can tell
> What his horny throat expresseth . . .

[5] Hampstead Keats. V.305.

> upon the meadow-grasses or young corn, not stirring till the flow of air was all around him.

Severn, who tended rather toward revery and vagueness, was repeatedly "astonished" at the closeness with which Keats would notice details, until Severn himself began to catch a little of it:

> Nothing seemed to escape him, the song of a bird and the undernote of response from covert or hedge, the rustle of some animal, the changing of the green and brown lights and furtive shadows, the motions of the wind—just how it took certain tall flowers and plants—and the wayfaring of the clouds: even the features and gestures of passing tramps, the colour of one woman's hair, the smile on one child's face, the furtive animalism below the deceptive humanity in many of the vagrants, even the hats, clothes, shoes, wherever these conveyed the remotest hint as to the real self of the wearer.

Severn's notice of Keats's delight in whatever conveyed "the remotest hint as to the real self of the wearer" carries us forward to the Chaucerian relish of character that we find increasingly in the longer letters and even in the mere underlinings and marginal notes of Keats's reading. "Scenery is fine," he writes to Bailey (March 13, 1818), "but human nature is finer —The Sward is richer for the tread of a real, nervous [E]nglish foot." Reading a month or so later in an old copy (1634) of Mateo Aleman's *The Rogue: or, the Life of Guzman de Alfarache,* which James Rice had just given him, he underlines the words, "his voice lowd and shrill but not very cleere," and writes in the margin: "This puts me in mind of Fielding's Fanny 'whose teeth were white but uneven'; it is the same sort of personality. The great Man in this way is Chaucer."

VI

A fairly large internal fund was thus available to be tapped when Keats read, undoubtedly at Bailey's suggestion, Hazlitt's *Essay on the Principles of Human Action,* and bought a copy that was still in his library at his death.

Hazlitt's aim in this short book—his first published work—was to refute the contention of Thomas Hobbes and his eighteenth century followers that self-love, in one way or another, is the mainspring of all human action, and to prove instead, as the subtitle states, "the Natural Disinterestedness of the Human Mind." Since British philosophy for a century had devoted more speculation to this problem than to any other, Hazlitt's youthful aim was quite ambitious (he began the book in his early twenties, and was twenty-seven when it appeared). His procedure was ingenious, and to some extent original. Moralists trying to disprove Hobbes had for fifty years or more been stressing the sympathetic potentialities of the imagination. Adam Smith's influential *Theory of Moral Sentiments* (1759) is the best-known example. The interest spread to the critical theory of the arts; and well over a century before German psychology developed the theory of *Einfühlung*—for which the word "empathy" was later coined as a translation—English critical theory had anticipated many of the insights involved.[6] It was the peculiar fate of many psychological discoveries of the English eighteenth century to be forgotten from the 1830s until the hungry theorization of the German universities in the late nineteenth century led to a rediscovery and a more systematized and subjective interpretation.

In his *Principles of Human Action,* Hazlitt went much further than Adam Smith's *Theory of Moral Sentiments.* His hope was to show that imaginative sympathy was not a mere escape hatch from the prison of egocentricity, but something thoroughgoing, something indigenous and inseparable from all activities of the mind. Sympathetic identification takes place constantly—even if only with ourselves and our own desired future. Hazlitt's psychology, in effect, is a more dynamic version of Locke's. Instead of the image of the mind as a *tabula rasa* on which experience writes, we have an image of it as something more actively adhesive and projective: equally dependent on what is outside itself for its own coloration, so to speak, but actively uniting with its objects, growing, dwindling, even becoming poisoned, by what it assimilates. Hazlitt's argument turns on the nature of "identity." Suppose that I love myself in the thoroughgoing way that the Hobbists claim—that everything I do, or plan, or hope, is in order to help myself or avoid pain in the future: that even what we call generous acts are done solely (as the Hobbists

[6] A brief discussion of the subject as it applies to eighteenth-century literary criticism may be found in *From Classic to Romantic* (1946) by the present writer, pp. 131-147, 153-156. The theory of *Einfühlung,* developed by Lotze and later the school of Wundt, and treated most fully in the *Ästhetik* (1903-1906) of Theodor Lipps, was more subjective in its premise: it signified less an actual participation in the object—less of an objective coloring of the mind by the object—than the attribution to it of qualities and responses peculiar to the imagination itself. The insight, in other words, though accompanied by the merging of the perceiving mind and the perceived object, is largely the by-product of the working of the imagination, projected upon the object. This restriction of *Einfühlung* is extended even more in the strict interpretation of "empathy" —the English equivalent popularized by Vernon Lee in 1912, and first supplied in 1909 by E. B. Titchener, a pupil of Wundt.

maintained) because I wish to be praised, or because I wish to get along with others, or because I wish—at least—to be able to live with myself. But how can I know, how especially can I "love," this "identity" that I consider myself? If we look at the problem with empirical honesty, we have to admit that any feeling we have that we are one person, the same person, from one moment to the next (that we have, in short, an "identity") comes directly through two means only—"sensation" and "memory." A child who has burned his finger knows only through "sensation" that it is he and not someone else who has done so. In a similar way, he knows only through "memory" that it was he and not someone else who had this experience in the past. If our identities until now depend on sensation and memory, what can give me an interest in my future sensations? Sensation and memory are not enough. I can picture my future identity only through my *imagination*. The child who has been burned will dread the prospect of future pain from the fire because, through his imagination, he "projects himself forward into the future, and identifies himself with his future being." His imagination "creates" his own future to him.

In short, I can "abstract myself from my present being and take an interest in my future being [only] in the same sense and manner, in which I can go out of myself entirely and enter into the minds and feelings of others." The capacity for imaginative identification, in other words, is not instinctively or mechanically obliged to turn in one direction rather than another: the sole means by which "I can anticipate future objects, or be interested in them," throwing "me forward as it were into my future being" and anticipating events that do not yet exist, is equally able to "carry me out of myself into the feelings of others by one and the same process . . . I could not love myself, if I were not capable of loving others." If stronger ideas than those of one's own identity are present to the mind, the imagination can turn more easily to them. Hazlitt here develops the belief of the associationist psychologists of the time, in whom he was widely read, that the mind instinctively follows and "imitates" what is before it. . . .

The argument for "the natural disinterestedness of the mind" is not, of course, that most people are really disinterested, but that there is no mechanical determinism, such as Hobbes and his followers assumed, toward self-love. The disinterestedness exists as far as the *potential* development of the mind is concerned. Knowledge can direct and habituate the imagination to ideas other than that of our own identity. We commonly see that long acquaintance with another increases our sympathy, provided undesirable qualities in the other person, or sheer monotony, do not work against it. If the child is unsympathetic to others, it is not from automatic self-love but because of lack of knowledge—a lack that also prevents him from identifying himself very successfully with his own future interests. Greatness in art, philosophy, moral action—the "heroic" in any sense—involves losing the sense of "our personal identity in some object dearer to us than ourselves." . . .

VII

Less than three weeks after Keats wrote the "Negative Capability" letter to his brothers around Christmastime, Hazlitt began a course of lectures at the Surrey Institution, just south of Blackfriars Bridge, every Tuesday evening at seven o'clock. These were the famous *Lectures on the English Poets,* the first of which was on January 13 and the last on March 3. Keats looked forward to hearing them all, and, as far as we know, missed only one ("On Chaucer and Spenser," January 20), when he arrived too late. A few sentences at the start of the third lecture, "On Shakespeare and Milton" (January 27), which Keats told Bailey he definitely planned to attend, may have especially struck him. Shakespeare, said Hazlitt,

> was the least of an egotist that it was possible to be. He was nothing in himself; but he was all that others were, or that they could become. He not only had in himself the germs of every faculty and feeling, but he could follow them by anticipation, intuitively, into all their conceivable ramifications, through every change of fortune, or conflict of passion, or turn of thought. . . . He had only to think of anything in order to become that thing, with all the circumstances belonging to it.

By contrast, much modern poetry seems to have become engaged in a competition to "reduce" itself "to a mere effusion of natural sensibility," surrounding "the meanest objects with the morbid feelings and devouring egotism of the writers' own minds."

The immediate effect of Hazlitt's lectures was to open Keats's eyes much sooner than would otherwise have happened to the limitations of the prevailing modes of poetry—limitations that were far from obvious to most writers until a full century had run its course. But the ideal of the "characterless" poet, touching as it did qualities and habits of response intrinsic to himself, gradually took a secure hold of his imagination throughout the months ahead, though still later it was to appear to him as something of an oversimplification. The extent to which it became domesticated in his habitual thinking is shown by a letter the following autumn, at the beginning of the astonishing year (October 1818 to October 1819) when his greatest poetry was written. He is writing to Richard Woodhouse (October 27):

> As to the poetical Character itself (I mean that sort of which, if I am anything, I am a Member; that sort distinguished from the wordworthian or egotistical sublime; which is a thing per se and stands alone) it is not itself —it has no self—it is everything and nothing—It has no character—it enjoys light and shade; it lives in gusto, be it foul or fair, high or low, rich or poor, mean or elevated—It has as much delight in conceiving an Iago as an Imogen. What shocks the virtuous philosop[h]er, delights the camelion Poet. It does no harm from its relish of the dark side of things any more than from its taste for the bright one; because they both end in speculation. A Poet is the most unpoetical of any thing in existence; because he has no Identity —he is continually in for—and filling some other Body—The Sun, the Moon, the Sea and Men and Women who are creatures of impulse are poetical and have about them an unchangeable attribute—the poet has none; no identity—he is certainly the most unpoetical of all God's Creatures. . . . When I am in a room with People if I ever am free from speculating on creations of my own brain, then not myself goes home to myself: but the identity of every one in the room begins to press upon me [so] that I am in a very little time annihilated—not only among Men; it would be the same in a Nursery of children.

Woodhouse, who by now had acquired a close knowledge of Keats, found these remarks a good description of Keats's own bent of mind, and wrote to John Taylor,

> I believe him to be right with regard to his own Poetical Character—And I perceive clearly the distinction between himself & those of the Wordsworth School. . . . The highest order of Poet will not only possess all the above powers but will have [so] high an imag^{n} that he will be able to throw his own soul into any object he sees or imagines, so as to see feel be sensible of, & express, all that the object itself wo^{d} see feel be sensible of or express—& he will speak out of that object—so that his own self will with the Exception of the Mechanical part be "annihilated."—and it is [of] the excess of this power that I suppose Keats to speak, when he says he has no identity—As a poet, and when the fit is upon him, this is true. . . . Shakesp^{r} was a poet of the kind above ment^{d}—and he was perhaps the only one besides Keats who possessed this power in an extr^{y} degree.

Keats had talked with Woodhouse about the subject before, and had thrown himself into it with the fanciful exuberance he found irresistible when he was among serious people. For Woodhouse adds the comment noticed earlier: "He has affirmed that he can conceive of a billiard Ball that it may have a sense of delight from its own roundness, smoothness volubility & the rapidity of its motion." [7]

VIII

We have been anticipating, of course: the implications of the "Negative Capability" letter have encouraged us to look ahead a few months. Back in December, as he felt himself emerging onto this new plateau of thinking, the memory of *King Lear* kept recurring. When he had begun *Endymion* at the Isle of Wight, it was the sea—remembered from the cliff near Margate the summer before (1816)—that had led him to return to the play on this second venture: "the passage . . . 'Do you not hear the Sea?' has haunted me intensely." Now that *Endymion* was finished, and a third venture or transition lay ahead, he was remembering the play somewhat differently. It was probably in December, certainly by early January, that he bought a copy of Hazlitt's *Characters of Shakespear's Plays* (published late in 1817). With only one exception, all his underscorings and marginal comments are concentrated in the chapter on *Lear*.[8] They provide in their own way a further gloss to that "intensity" of conception—that identification and "greeting of the Spirit"—of which he had been thinking when he wrote to George and Tom ("Examine King Lear & you will find this exemplified throughout"): an identification especially prized when—as Hazlitt said in a passage Keats underlines —"the extremest resources of the imagination are called in to lay open the deepest movements of the heart." "The greatest strength of genius," said Hazlitt, "is shown in describing the strongest passions: for the power of the imagination, in works of invention, must be in proportion to the force of the natural impressions, which are the subject of them." Double-scoring this in the margin, Keats writes:

> If we compare the Passions to different tuns and hogsheads of wine in a vast cellar—thus it is—the poet by one cup should know the scope of any particular wine without getting intoxicated—this is the highest exertion of Power, and the next step is to paint from memory of gone self storms.

[7] *Keats Circle,* I.57-60. When he was preparing to leave Margate for Canterbury, after beginning *Endymion,* he hoped "the Rememberance of Chaucer will set me forward like a Billiard-Ball" (I.147).

[8] Harvard Keats Collection. Marked passages and comments are printed in Lowell, II.587-590, and Hampstead Keats, V.280-286.

And beside another passage he draws a line, underscoring the italicized words, and writes "This passage has to a great degree hieroglyphic visioning":

> We see the ebb and flow of the feeling, its pauses and feverish starts, its impatience of opposition, its accumulating force when it has time to recollect itself, *the manner in which it avails itself of every passing word or gesture, its haste to repel insinuation, the alternate contradiction and dilatation of the soul.*

Endymion, which he began to copy and correct for the press during the first week of January, seemed remote indeed from the thoughts that now preoccupied him. So in fact did romances generally, though he was to write two more (*Isabella* and *The Eve of St. Agnes*). On Thursday, January 22, he finished copying the first book of *Endymion;* and then, as he told his brothers the next day, "I sat down . . . to read King Lear once again the thing appeared to demand the prologue of a Sonnet, I wrote it & began to read." It is hardly one of his best sonnets—he never even bothered to publish it—but the occasion meant something to him. For he was approaching the play with a new understanding of how much lay beyond the "old oak Forest" of "Romance."

It was only another beginning, and it would have to proceed much more slowly than the other beginnings. But he was prepared, he thought, for "a very gradual ripening of the intellectual powers"; and all he can say now is that "I think a little change has taken place in my intellect lately." Then he turns to the sonnet, copies it out for George and Tom, and adds: "So you see I am getting at it, with a sort of determination & strength, though verily I do not feel it at this moment—this is my fourth letter this morning & I feel rather tired & my head rather swimming."

II

Discussions of Particular Poems

The Hoodwinking of Madeline: Scepticism in *The Eve of St. Agnes*

by Jack Stillinger

I

The commonest response to *The Eve of St. Agnes* has been the celebration of its "heady and perfumed loveliness." The poem has been called "a monody of dreamy richness," "one long sensuous utterance," "an expression of lyrical emotion," "a great affirmation of love," "a great choral hymn," an expression of "unquestioning rapture," and many things else. Remarks like these tend to confirm one's uneasy feeling that what is sometimes called "the most perfect" of Keats's longer poems is a mere fairy-tale romance, unhappily short on meaning. For many readers, as for Douglas Bush, the poem is "no more than a romantic tapestry of unique richness of color"; one is "moved less by the experience of the characters than . . . by the incidental and innumerable beauties of descriptive phrase and rhythm." [1]

To be sure, not all critics have merely praised Keats's pictures. After all, the poem opens on a note of "bitter chill," and progresses through images of cold and death before the action gets under way. When young Porphyro comes from across the moors to claim his bride, he enters a

"The Hoodwinking of Madeline: Scepticism in *The Eve of St. Agnes*" by Jack Stillinger. From *Studies in Philology*, LVIII (1961). Reprinted by permission of the author, who has made some deletions for the present volume.

[1] John Keats, *Selected Poems and Letters* (Boston, 1959), pp. xvi, 333; see also Bush's "Keats and His Ideas," in *The Major English Romantic Poets: A Symposium in Reappraisal*, ed. Clarence D. Thorpe, et al. (Carbondale, Ill., 1957), pp. 239 f. The view is sanctioned by Keats himself, who thought the poem was in some ways like "Isabella"—"too smokeable," with "too much inexperience of . . . [life], and simplicity of knowledge in it," "A weak-sided Poem"; when he later planned a new attempt in poetry, it was "the colouring of St Agnes eve" that he would "diffuse . . . throughout a Poem in which Character and Sentiment would be the figures to such drapery" (*The Letters of John Keats*, ed. Hyder E. Rollins, Cambridge, Mass., 1958, II, 174, 234).

hostile castle, where Madeline's kinsmen will murder even upon holy days; and in the face of this danger he proceeds to Madeline's bedchamber. With the sexual consummation of their love, a storm comes up, and they must escape the castle, past "sleeping dragons," porter, and bloodhound, out into the night. The ending reverts to the opening notes of bitter chill and death: Madeline's kinsmen are benightmared, the old Beadsman and Madeline's nurse Angela are grotesquely dispatched into the next world. Some obvious contrasts are made in the poem: the lovers' youth and vitality are set against the old age and death associated with Angela and the Beadsman; the warmth and security of Madeline's chamber are contrasted with the coldness and hostility of the rest of the castle and the icy storm outside; the innocence and purity of young love are played off against the sensuousness of the revellers elsewhere in the castle; and so on. Through these contrasts, says one critic, Keats created a tale of young love "not by forgetting what everyday existence is like, but by using the mean, sordid, and commonplace as a foundation upon which to build a high romance"; the result is no mere fairy tale, but a poem that "has a rounded fulness, a complexity and seriousness, a balance which remove it from the realm of mere magnificent tour de force." [2]

But still something is wanting. The realistic notes all seem to ocur in the framework, and the main action is all romance. There is no interaction between the contrasting elements, and hence no conflict. Porphyro is never really felt to be in danger; through much of the poem the lovers are secluded from the rest of the world; and at the end, when they escape, they meet no obstacle, but rather "glide, like phantoms, into the wide hall; / Like phantoms, to the iron porch, they glide. . . . By one, and one, the bolts full easy slide:— / The chains lie silent . . . The key turns . . . the door upon its hinges groans. / And they are gone" (361-370). It is all too easy. Though the poem ends with the nightmares of the warriors, and the deaths of Angela and the Beadsman, the lovers seem untouched, for they have already fled the castle. And besides, this all happened "ages long ago" (370). We are back where we started, with a fairy-tale romance, unhappily short on meaning.

The only serious attempt to make something of the poem has come from a small group of critics whom I shall call "metaphysical critics" because they think Keats was a metaphysician. To them the poem seems to dramatize certain ideas that Keats held a year or two earlier about the nature of the imagination, the relationship between this world and the next, and the progress of an individual's ascent toward spiritualization.

[2] R. H. Fogle, "A Reading of Keats's 'Eve of St. Agnes.'" *CE*, VI (1945), 328, 325.

According to the popular superstition connected with St. Agnes' Eve, a young maiden who fasts and neither speaks nor looks about before she goes to bed may get sight of her future husband in a dream. Madeline follows this prescription, dreams of her lover, then seems to awaken out of her dream to find him present in her chamber, an actual, physical fact. Her dream in a sense comes true. The events are thought to relate to a passage in the well-known letter to Benjamin Bailey, 22 November 1817, in which Keats expressed his faith in "the truth of Imagination": "What the imagination seizes as Beauty must be truth—whether it existed before or not. . . . The Imagination may be compared to Adam's dream—he awoke and found it truth." For the metaphysical critics, just as Adam dreamed of the creation of Eve, then awoke to find his dream a truth—Eve before him a beautiful reality—so Madeline dreams of Porphyro and awakens to find him present and palpably real.

But the imagination is not merely prophetic: it is "a Shadow of reality to come" hereafter; and in the same letter Keats is led on to "another favorite Speculation"—"that we shall enjoy ourselves hereafter by having what we called happiness on Earth repeated in a finer tone and so repeated. . . . Adam's dream will do here and seems to be a conviction that Imagination and its empyreal reflection is the same as human Life and its spiritual repetition." The idea is that a trust in the visionary imagination will allow us to "burst our mortal bars," to "dodge / Conception to the very bourne of heaven," to transcend our earthly confines, guess at heaven, and arrive at some view of the reality to come. If the visionary imagination is valid, the earthly pleasures portrayed in our visions will make up our immortal existence—will be spiritually "repeated in a finer tone and so repeated."

In this sense, Madeline's dream of Porphyro is a case history in the visionary imagination. According to the metaphysical critics, she is, in her dream, at heaven's bourne, already enjoying a kind of spiritual repetition of earthly happiness. On being roused by Porphyro, she finds in him "a painful change" (300): "How chang'd thou art! how pallid, chill, and drear!" she says to him; "Give me that voice again . . . Those looks immortal" (311-313). Porphyro's reply takes the form of action: "Beyond a mortal man impassion'd far / At these voluptuous accents, he arose" (316 f.). He transcends his mortal existence, joins Madeline at heaven's bourne by melting into her dream, and together they store up pleasures to be immortally repeated in a finer tone.

The other main strand of the critics' thinking concerns the apotheosis of Porphyro. By relating the poem to Keats's simile of human life as a

"Mansion of Many Apartments," the critics would persuade us that the castle of Madeline's kinsmen allegorically represents human life, and that Porphyro, passing upward to a closet adjoining Madeline's bedchamber, and thence into the chamber itself, progresses from apartment to apartment in the mansion of life, executing a spiritual ascent to heaven's bourne. For a number of reasons, Keats's simile confuses rather than clarifies the poem.[3] But the idea of spiritual pilgrimage is not entirely to be denied. Porphyro says to the sleeping Madeline, "Thou art my heaven, and I thine eremite" (277), and when she awakens, after the consummation, he exclaims to her: "Ah, silver shrine, here will I take my rest / After so many hours of toil and quest, / A famish'd pilgrim,—saved by miracle" (337-339).

In brief summary, the main points of the metaphysical critics' interpretation are that Madeline's awakening to find Porphyro in her bedroom is a document in the validity of the visionary imagination; that Porphyro in the course of the poem makes a spiritual pilgrimage, ascending higher by stages until he arrives at transcendant reality in Madeline's bed; and that there the lovers re-enact earthly pleasures that will be stored up for further, still more elevated repetition in a finer tone. If these ideas seem farfetched and confused, the fact should be attributed in part to the brevity of my exposition, and to the shortcomings of any attempt to abstract ideas from a complicated poem, even when it is treated as allegory. Yet one may suggest reasons for hesitating to accept them.

For one thing, when the imaginative vision of beauty turns out to be a truth—when Madeline awakens to find Porphyro in her bed—she is not nearly so pleased as Adam was when he awoke and discovered Eve. In fact, truth here is seemingly undersirable: Madeline is frightened out of her wits, and she laments, "No dream, alas! alas! and woe is mine! / Porphyro will leave me here to fade and pine" (328 f.). For another, it is a reversal of Keats's own sequence to find in the poem the spiritual repetition of earthly pleasures. In Madeline's dream the imaginative enactment of pleasure comes first; it is an earthly repetition of spiritual pleasure that follows, and perhaps in a grosser, rather than a finer, tone. That the lovers are consciously intent on experiencing the conditions of immor-

[3] The simile occurs in a letter to J. H. Reynolds, 3 May 1818 (*Letters,* I, 280 f.). Porphyro's eagerness to get to Madeline hardly accords with Keats's idea that "we care not to hasten" to "the second Chamber"; the identification of Madeline's bedroom with "the Chamber of Maiden-Thought" seems similarly unfitting, since one of the effects of and nature of Man—of convincing ones nerves that the World is full of Misery and arriving in the latter is "that tremendous one of sharpening one's vision into the heart Heartbreak, Pain, Sickness and oppression."

tality—consciously practising for the spiritual repetition of pleasure at an even higher level of intensity—implies, if one reads the critics correctly, that both Madeline and Porphyro have read *Endymion,* Keats's letters, and the explications of the metaphysical critics.

Much of the critics' interpretation rests on the religious language of the poem. Madeline is "St. Agnes' charmed maid," "a mission'd spirit" (192 f.), "all akin / To spirits of the air" (201 f.), "a saint," "a splendid angel, newly drest, / Save wings, for heaven," "so pure a thing, so free from mortal taint" (222-225). To Porphyro, her "eremite," she is "heaven" (277), and from closet to bedchamber he progresses from purgatory to paradise. Finally, Porphyro is "A famish'd pilgrim,—saved by miracle" (339). But the significance of such language is questionable. In *Romeo and Juliet,* with which *The Eve of St. Agnes* has much in common, Juliet's hand at the first meeting of the lovers is a "holy shrine," and Romeo's lips are "two blushing pilgrims"; subsequently Juliet is a "dear saint," a "bright angel," a "fair saint"; "heaven is . . . Where Juliet lives," and outside Verona is "purgatory, torture, hell itself"; she is compared to a "winged messenger of heaven," and her lips carry "immortal blessing." At the same time Romeo is "the god of . . . [Juliet's] idolatry," and a "mortal paradise of . . . sweet flesh." [4] In other poems Keats himself, in the manner of hundreds of poets before him, uses religious terms in hyperbolic love language: for example, Isabella's lover Lorenzo is called "a young palmer in Love's eye," he is said to "shrive" his passion, and (in a stanza ultimately rejected from the poem) he declares that he would be "full deified" by the gift of a love token.[5]

What is perhaps most telling against the critics, in connection with the religious language of *The Eve of St. Agnes,* is that when Porphyro calls himself "A famish'd pilgrim,—saved by miracle," his words must be taken ironically, unless Keats has forgotten, or hopes the reader has forgotten, all the action leading to the consummation. The miracle on which Porphyro congratulates himself is in fact a *stratagem* that he has planned and carried out to perfection. Early in the poem, when he first encounters Angela, she is amazed to see him, and says that he "must hold water in a witch's sieve, / And be liege-lord of all the Elves and Fays, / To venture" into a castle of enemies (120-122). Although Porphyro later assures Madeline that he is "no rude infidel" (342), the images in Angela's speech

[4] I. v. 96 f., 105; II. ii. 26, 55, 61; III. iii. 29 f., 18; II. ii. 28; III. iii. 37; II ii. 114; III. ii. 82.

[5] Lines 2, 64, and the rejected stanza following line 56 (*The Poetical Works of John Keats,* ed. H. W. Garrod, 2nd edn., Oxford, 1958, p. 217 n.).

tend to link him with witches and fairies rather than with the Christian pilgrim. By taking a closer look at the poem, we may see that Keats had misgivings about Porphyro's fitness to perform a spiritual pilgrimage and arrive at heaven.

II

Porphyro's first request of Angela, "Now tell me where is Madeline" (114), is followed by an oath upon the holy loom used to weave St. Agnes' wool, and it is implied that he is well aware what night it is. "St. Agnes' Eve," says Angela, "God's help! my lady fair the conjuror plays / This very night: good angels her deceive!" (123-125). While she laughs at Madeline's folly, Porphyro gazes on her, until "Sudden a thought came like a full-blown rose. . . . then doth he propose / A stratagem" (136-139). The full force of "stratagem" comes to be felt in the poem—a ruse, an artifice, a trick for deceiving. For Angela, the deception of Madeline by good angels is funny; but Porphyro's is another kind of deception, and no laughing matter. She is startled, and calls him "cruel," "impious," "wicked" (140, 143); the harshness of the last line of her speech emphasizes her reaction: "Thou canst not surely be the same that thou didst seem" (144).

Porphyro swears "by all saints" not to harm Madeline: "O may I ne'er find grace / When my weak voice shall whisper its last prayer, / If one of her soft ringlets I displace" (145-148). He next enforces his promise with a suicidal threat: Angela must believe him, or he "will . . . Awake, with horrid shout" his foemen, "And beard them" (151-153). Because Angela is "A poor, weak, palsy-stricken, churchyard thing" (155), she presently accedes, promising to do whatever Porphyro wishes—

> Which was, to lead him, in close secrecy,
> Even to Madeline's chamber, and there hide
> Him in a closet, of such privacy
> That he might see her beauty unespied,
> And win perhaps that night a peerless bride,
> While legion'd fairies pac'd the coverlet,
> And pale enchantment held her sleepy-eyed. (163-169)

At this point our disbelief must be suspended if we are to read the poem as an affirmation of romantic love. We must leave our world behind, where stratagems like Porphyro's are frowned on, sometimes punished in the criminal courts, and enter an imaginary world where "in sooth such things have been" (81). But the narrator's summary comment on the stratagem is that "Never on such a night have lovers met, / Since Merlin paid his Demon all the monstrous debt" (170 f.). The allusion is puzzling. Commentators feel that the "monstrous debt" is Merlin's debt to his demon-father for his own life, and that he paid it by committing evil deeds, or perhaps specifically by effecting his own imprisonment and death through the misworking of a spell. However it is explained, it strengthens rather than dispels our suspicion, like Angela's, that Porphyro is up to no good; and, with the earlier images of "legion'd fairies" and "pale enchantment," it brings further associations of fairy-lore and sorcery to bear on his actions. Then Angela asserts a kind of orthodox middle-class morality: "Ah! thou must needs the lady wed" (179).

She now leads Porphyro to Madeline's chamber, "silken, hush'd, and chaste," where he takes "covert'" (187 f.). In the first draft Stanza XXI is incomplete, but two versions that can be pieced together call Porphyro's hiding-place "A purgatory sweet to view love's own domain" and "A purgatory sweet to what may he attain." The rejected lines, mentioning "purgatory sweet" as a stage toward the "paradise" (244) of Madeline's chamber, are documents in Porphyro's spiritual pilgrimage, perhaps. The ideas of viewing love's own domain, or what he may attain, are documents in the peeping-Tomism that occupies the next few stanzas. As Angela is feeling her way toward the stair, she is met by Madeline, who turns back to help her down to "a safe level matting" (196). If the action is significant, its meaning lies in the juxtaposition of Madeline's unselfish act of "pious care" (194) with the leering overtones just before of Porphyro's having hidden himself in her closet, "pleas'd amain" (188)—pleased exceedingly by the success of his stratagem—and with the tone of the narrator's words immediately following: "Now prepare, / Young Porphyro, for gazing on that bed; / She comes, she comes again, like ring-dove fray'd and fled" (196-198).

The mention of "ring-dove" is interesting. Porphyro has taken "covert" —the position of the hunter (or perhaps merely the bird-watcher). There follows a series of bird images that perhaps may be thought of in terms of the hunter's game. In a variant to the stanza Madeline is "an affrighted Swan"; here she is a "ring-dove"; in the next stanza her heart is "a tongueless nightingale" (206); later in the poem she is "A dove forlorn" (333); still later Porphyro speaks of robbing her nest (340), and in a variant says, "Soft Nightingale, I'll keep thee in a cage / To sing to me." [6] It is un-

[6] For the variants see Garrod, pp. 245 n., 253 n.

likely that all these images carry connotations of hunting, nest-robbing, and caging; Romeo will "climb a bird's nest" when he ascends the ladder to Juliet's room (II. v. 76). But the single comparison of Madeline's heart to a "tongueless nightingale" seems significant. Leigh Hunt naturally missed the point: "The nightingale! how touching the simile! the heart a 'tongueless nightingale,' dying in that dell of the bosom. What thorough sweetness, and perfection of lovely imagery!" Critics pointing to Sotheby's translation of Wieland's *Oberon* (VI. 17), or to *Troilus and Criseyde* (III. 1233-39),[7] may also have missed the significance. For Keats's image embraces the entire story of the rape of Philomel, and with it he introduces a further note of evil that prevents us from losing ourselves in the special morality of fairy romance. Madeline has the status of one of St. Agnes' "lambs unshorn" (71); she is a maiden innocent and pure, but also is about to lose that status through what is in some ways a cruel deception. The comparison with Philomel is not inappropriate.

In Stanza XXV, as Madeline is described kneeling, we are told that "Porphyro grew faint: / She knelt, so pure a thing, so free from mortal taint" (224 f.). Though many reasons will suggest themselves why Porphyro grows faint, a novel one may be offered here. In his copy of *The Anatomy of Melancholy,* after a passage in which Burton tells how "The Barbarians stand in awe of a fair woman, and at a beautiful aspect, a fierce spirit is pacified," Keats wrote, "abash'd the devil stood." He quotes from Book IV of *Paradise Lost,* where Satan is confronted by the beautiful angel Zephon: "Abasht the Devil stood, / And felt how awful goodness is, and saw / Virtue in her shape how lovely, saw, and pin'd / His loss" (846-849). But since Burton speaks of standing "in awe of a fair woman" Keats must also have recalled Book IX, in which Satan's malice is momentarily overawed by Eve's graceful innocence: "That space the Evil one abstracted stood / From his own evil, and for the time remain'd / Stupidly good" (463-465). Porphyro's faintness may in some way parallel Satan's moment of stupid goodness. "But the hot Hell that always in him burns" soon ends Satan's relapse from evil intent, as he goes about Eve's ruin. So with Porphyro; for "Anon his heart revives" (226), as he pursues the working-out of his stratagem.

Madeline undresses, then falls fast asleep. Porphyro creeps to the bed, "Noiseless as fear in a wide wilderness" (250), and " 'tween the curtains peep'd, where, lo!—how fast she slept" (252). At the bedside he sets a table, when, in the midst of his preparations, a hall-door opens in the

[7] *Leigh Hunt's London Journal,* II (1835), 18; Sidney Colvin, *John Keats* (New York, 1925), p. 87 n.; F. E. L. Priesteley, "Keats and Chaucer," *MLQ,* V (1944), 444.

castle, and the revellers' music shatters the silence of the room. Porphyro calls for a "drowsy Morphean amulet" (257—and then "The hall door shuts . . . and all the noise is gone" (261). Madeline continues sleeping, while he brings from the closet the feast of candied apple, quince, plum, and all the rest.

Aside from the unheroic implications of "Noiseless as fear in a wide wilderness" and of the word "peep'd," there are three things worth noting in the stanzas just summarized. One is the relationship the poem has at this point with *Cymbeline,* II. ii. 11-50, in which the villainous Iachimo emerges from the trunk, where he has hidden himself, to gaze on the sleeping Imogen. Readers since Swinburne have noted resemblances. Imogen is "a heavenly angel," and like Madeline a "fresh lily," "whiter than the sheets," as she lies in bed, sleeping, in effect, an "azure-lidded sleep" (262)—and so on. But no critic has been willing to include among the resemblances that Porphyro's counterpart in the scene is a villain. In the speech from which these details have been drawn, Iachimo compares himself with Tarquin, who raped Lucrece, and he notes that Imogen "hath been reading late / The tale of Tereus; here the leaf's turn'd down / Where Philomel gave up."

The second point concerns Porphyro's call for a "drowsy Morphean amulet"—a sleep-inducing charm to prevent Madeline's awakening when the music bursts forth into the room. Earlier he has wished to win Madeline while "pale enchantment held her sleepy-eyed" (169). Here he would assist "pale enchantment" with a "Morphean amulet." It may not be amiss to recall Lovelace, and the stratagem by which he robbed Clarissa of her maidenhood. "I know thou wilt blame me for having had recourse to *Art,*" writes Lovelace to John Belford, in Richardson's novel. "But do not physicians prescribe opiates in acute cases." Besides, "a Rape, thou knowest, to us Rakes, is far from being an undesirable thing."[8]

The third point concerns the feast that Porphyro sets out. In his copy of *The Anatomy of Melancholy,* opposite a passage in which Burton commends fasting as an excellent means of preparation for devotion, "by which chast thoughts are ingendred . . . concupiscence is restrained, vicious . . . lusts and humours are expelled," Keats recorded his approval in the marginal comment "good." It is for some reason of this sort that Madeline fasts, going "supperless to bed" (51). Porphyro's feast seems intended to produce the opposite results, and there is more than a suggestion of pagan sensuality in the strange affair of eastern luxuries that

[8] *Clarissa,* Shakespeare Head edn. (Oxford, 1930), V, 339 f.

he heaps as if by magic—"with glowing hand" (271)—on the table by the bed.

Next Porphyro tries to awaken Madeline, or so it seems: "And now, my love, my seraph fair, awake! / Thou art my heaven, and I thine eremite" (276 f.). The last line carries the suggestion that Porphyro has been reading of the martyrdom, not of St. Agnes, but of Donne's lovers in "The Canonization," whose bodies are by "reverend love" made "one another's hermitage." It is curious that in the proposition that follows, "Open thine eyes . . . Or I shall drowse beside thee" (278 f.), Porphyro does not wait for an answer: "Thus whispering, his warm, unnerved arm / Sank in her pillow" (280 f.). "Awakening up" (289), he takes Madeline's lute and plays an ancient ditty, which causes her to utter a soft moan. It would seem that she does at this point wake up: "Suddenly / Her blue affrayed eyes wide open shone. . . . Her eyes were open, but she still beheld, / Now wide awake, the vision of her sleep" (295-299). Not unreasonably, we might think, she weeps, sighs, and "moan[s] forth witless words" (303).

We shall see in a moment, however, that she has not after all awakened from her trance. The "painful change" she witnesses—the substitution of the genuine Porphyro for the immortal looks and voice of her vision—"*nigh* expell'd / The blisses of her dream" (300 f.), came near expelling them, but did not in fact do so. Apparently she is to be thought of as still in her trance, but capable of speaking to the Porphyro before her, when she says, "Ah, Porphyro! . . . but even now / Thy voice was at sweet tremble in mine ear" (307 f.). To her request for "that voice again . . . Those looks immortal" (312 f.), Porphyro offers neither, but rather impassioned action of godlike intensity. At the end of Stanza XXXVI, the image of "St. Agnes' moon" combines the notions of St. Agnes, the patron saint of maidenhood, and Cynthia, the goddess of chastity, and the symbolic combination has "set," gone out of the picture to be replaced by a storm: "Meantime the frost-wind blows / Like Love's alarum pattering the sharp sleet / Against the window-panes; St. Agnes' moon hath set" (322-324).

Keats's final manuscript version of the consummation, rejected by his publishers on moral grounds, as making the poem unfit to be read by young ladies, is more graphic. For a rather lame conclusion to Madeline's speech (314 f.), he substituted the lines, "See while she speaks his arms encroaching slow / Have zon'd her, heart to heart—loud, loud the dark winds blow." Then he rewrote Stanza XXXVI:

> For on the midnight came a tempest fell.
> More sooth for that his close rejoinder flows
> Into her burning ear;—and still the spell
> Unbroken guards her in serene repose.
> With her wild dream he mingled as a rose
> Marryeth its odour to a violet.
> Still, still she dreams—louder the frost wind blows
> Like Love's alarum pattering the sharp sleet
> Against the window-panes; St. Agnes' moon hath set.[9]

The revised version makes clearer that Madeline is still dreaming: "still the spell / Unbroken guards her in serene repose." And it makes clearer the connection between the sexual consummation, the setting of St. Agnes' moon, and the rising of the storm. When Porphyro's "close rejoinder flows / Into . . . [the] burning ear" of Madeline, we may or may not recall Satan "Squat like a Toad, close at the ear of *Eve*" (IV. 800); but one would go out of his way to avoid a parallel between the advent of the storm in Keats's poem and the change in Nature that comes about when our first mother in an evil hour reached forth and ate the fruit: "Earth felt the wound, and Nature from her seat / Sighing through all her Works gave signs of woe, / That all was lost" (IX. 782-784). Unlike Eve, however, rather more like Clarissa, Madeline by this time has no choice; the revision heightens the contrast between her innocent unconsciousness and the storm raging outside: "Still, still she dreams—louder the frost wind blows."

As printed, the poem continues " 'Tis dark: quick pattereth the flaw-blown sleet." Then Porphyro: "This is no dream, my bride, my Madeline!" Another line describes the storm: " 'Tis dark: the iced gusts still rave and beat" (325-327). And now Madeline finally does wake up, if she ever does. Her speech shows a mixed attitude toward what has happened,

[9] Garrod, p. 252 n. After hearing the revised version, Richard Woodhouse wrote to the publisher John Taylor, 19 September 1819, "I do apprehend it will render the poem unfit for ladies, & indeed scarcely to be mentioned to them among the 'things that are.' " Taylor replied six days later that if Keats "will not so far concede to my Wishes as to leave the passage as it originally stood, I must be content to admire his Poems with some other Imprint" (*Letters,* II, 163, 183). According to Woodhouse's note heading one of the transcripts of the poem, Keats "left it to his Publishers to adopt which [alterations] they pleased, & to revise the whole" (Garrod, p. xxxviii). Though the argument cannot be made here, there are grounds for urging that a new text be made, embodying revisions found in the late fair copy (Garrod's *E*) and those noticed as alterations (*w*) in the second Woodhouse transcript (W^2). See "The Text of 'The Eve of St. Agnes,' " *Studies in Bibliography,* XVI (1963), 207-212.

but above all it is the lament of the seduced maiden: "No dream, alas! alas! and woe is mine! / Porphyro will leave me here to fade and pine.— / Cruel! what traitor could thee hither bring?" (328-330). She will curse not, for her heart is lost in his, or, perhaps more accurately, still lost in her romantic idealization of him. But she is aware that her condition is woeful: Porphyro is cruel; Angela is a traitor; and Madeline is a "deceived thing;— / A dove forlorn and lost" (333). In subsequent stanzas Porphyro soothes her fears, again calls her his bride, and seems to make all wrongs right. He tells her that the storm outside is really only "an elfin-storm from faery land" (343), and that she should "Awake! arise! . . . and fearless be, / For o'er the southern moors I have a home for thee" (350 f.). They hurry out of the chamber, down the wide stairs, through the castle door—"And they are gone . . . fled away into the storm" (370 f.).

III

After giving so much space to Porphyro, in admittedly exaggerated fashion portraying him as peeping Tom and villainous seducer, I must now confess that I do not think his stratagem is the main concern of the poem. I have presented him as villain in order to suggest, in the first place, that he is not, after all, making a spiritual pilgrimage, unless the poem is to be read as a satire on spiritual pilgrimages; in the second place, that the lovers, far from being a single element in the poem, are as much protagonist and antagonist as Belinda and the Baron, or Clarissa and Lovelace; and in the third place, that no matter how much Keats entered into the feelings of his characters, he could not lose touch with the claims and responsibilities of the world he lived in.

Certainly he partially identified himself with Porphyro. When Woodhouse found his revisions objectionable, Keats replied that he should "despise a man who would be such an eunuch in sentiment as to leave a maid, with that Character about her, in such a situation: & sho[d] despise himself to write about it." One may cite the narrator's obvious relish in Porphyro's situation as Madeline is about to undress—"Now prepare, / Young Porphyro, for gazing on that bed" (196 f.)—and Keats's later objection to the poem that "in my dramatic capacity I enter fully into the feeling: but in Propria Persona I should be apt to quiz it myself." But sexual passion worried him: to Bailey he confessed in July 1818, "When I am among Women I have evil thoughts," and he wrote in his copy of

The Anatomy of Melancholy, "there is nothing disgraces me in my own eyes so much as being one of a race of eyes nose and mouth beings in a planet call'd the earth who . . . have always mingled goatish winnyish lustful love with the abstract adoration of the deity." Though it has touches of humor, *The Eve of St. Agnes* is a serious poem, regardless of the extent to which Keats identified with his hero, he introduced enough overtones of evil to make Porphyro's actions wrong within the structure of the poem.

From now on, however, it may be best to think of Porphyro as representing, like the storm that comes up simultaneously with his conquest, the ordinary cruelties of life in the world. Like Melville, Keats saw

> Too far into the sea; where every maw
> The greater on the less feeds evermore. . . .
> Still do I that most fierce destruction see,
> The Shark at savage prey—the hawk at pounce,
> The gentle Robin, like a pard or ounce,
> Ravening a worm.[10]

Let Porphyro represent one of the sharks under the surface. And to borrow another figure from Melville, let the main concern of the poem be the young Platonist dreaming at the masthead: one false step, his identity comes back in horror, and with a half-throttled shriek he drops through transparent air into the sea, no more to rise for ever. There are reasons why we ought not entirely to sympathize with Madeline. She is a victim of deception, to be sure, but of deception not so much by Porphyro as by herself and the superstition she trusts in. Madeline the self-hoodwinked dreamer is, I think, the main concern of the poem, and I shall spend some time documenting this notion and relating it to Keat's other important poems—all of which, in a sense, are about dreaming.

If we recall Keats's agnosticism, his sonnet "Written in Disgust of Vulgar Superstition" (Christianity), and his abuse in the *Letters* of "the pious frauds of Religion," we may be prepared to see a hoodwinked dreamer in the poem even before we meet Madeline. He is the old Beadsman, so engrossed in an ascetic ritual that he is sealed off from the joys of life. After saying his prayers, he turns first through a door leading to the noisy revelry upstairs. "But no. . . . The joys of all his life were said and sung: / His was a harsh penance on St. Agnes' Eve" (22-24). And so he goes another way, to sit among rough ashes, while the focus of the nar-

[10] "To J. H. Reynolds, Esq.," ll. 93-95, 102-105 (Garrod, p. 487).

rative proceeds through the door he first opened, and on into the assembly of revellers, where we are introduced to Madeline and the ritual she is intent on following. In the final manuscript version, between Stanzas VI and VII, Keats inserted an additional stanza on the ritual, in part to explain the feast that Porphyro sets out:

> 'Twas said her future lord would there appear
> Offering as sacrifice—all in the dream—
> Delicious food even to her lips brought near:
> Viands and wine and fruit and sugar'd cream,
> To touch her palate with the fine extreme
> Of relish: then soft music heard; and then
> More pleasure followed in a dizzy stream
> Palpable almost: then to wake again
> Warm in the virgin morn, no weeping Magdalen.[11]

Then the poem, as it was printed, continues describing Madeline, who scarcely hears the music, and, with eyes fixed on the floor, pays no attention to anyone around her.

Several things deserve notice. By brooding "all that wintry day, / On love, and wing'd St. Agnes' saintly care" (43 f.), and by setting herself apart from the revellers, Madeline presents an obvious parallel with the Beadsman. Both are concerned with prayer and an ascetic ritual; both are isolated from the crowd and from actuality. A second point is that the superstition is clearly an old wives' tale: Madeline follows the prescription that "she had heard old dames full many times declare" (45). It is called by the narrator a "whim": "Full of this whim was thoughtful Madeline" (55). The irony of the added stanza enforces the point. Madeline's pleasures turn out to be palpable in fact. When she awakens to find herself with Porphyro, she is anything but warm: rather, she wakes up to "flaw-blown sleet" and "iced gusts" (325, 327); it is no virgin morn for her; and she is a "weeping Magdalen," who cries, "alas! alas! and woe is mine!" (328). But at this point, early in the poem, "she saw not: her heart was otherwhere: / She sigh'd for Agnes' dreams, the sweetest of the year" (62 f.). Perfunctorily dancing along, she is said to be "Hoodwink'd with faery fancy; all amort, / Save to St. Agnes and her lambs unshorn" (70 f.).

The superstition is next mentioned when Angela tells that Madeline

[11] Garrod, p. 238 n. In Ben Jonson's quatrain, quoted by Hunt from Brand's *Popular Antiquities* and often cited in notes to Keats's poem, the assurance that the ritual produces "an *empty* dream" is worth recalling (*Leigh Hunt's London Journal,* II, 1835, 17).

"the conjuror plays / This very night: good angels her deceive!" (124 f.). Porphyro thinks of the ritual in terms of "enchantments cold" and "legends old" (134 f.). Proceeding to her chamber, Madeline is called "St. Agnes' charmed maid," "a mission'd spirit, unaware" (192 f.). When she undresses, "Half-hidden, like a mermaid in sea-weed" (231), she is perhaps linked briefly with the drowning Ophelia, whose spreading clothes momentarily support her "mermaid-like" upon the water; like Ophelia, she is engrossed in a franciful dream-world.[12] "Pensive awhile she dreams awake, and sees, / In fancy, fair St. Agnes in her bed, / But dares not look behind, or all the charm is fled" (232-234). This last line carries a double meaning: in following her ritual, Madeline must look neither "behind, nor sideways" (53); but the real point is that if she did look behind, she would discover Porphyro, and then "the charm" would be "fled" for a more immediate reason.

Asleep in bed, Madeline is said to be "Blissfully haven'd both from joy and pain . . . Blinded alike from sunshine and from rain, / As though a rose should shut, and be a bud again" (240-243). Her dream is "a midnight charm / Impossible to melt as iced stream," "a stedfast spell" (282 f., 287). It is while she is in this state of stuporous insensibility—while "still the spell / Unbroken guards her in serene repose," "Still, still she dreams—louder the frost wind blows"—that Porphyro make love to her. On awakening to learn, "No dream, alas! alas! and woe is mine," she calls herself "a deceived thing," echoing Angela's words earlier, "good angels her deceive!" Her condition is pitiful, yet at the same time reprehensible. Her conjuring (perhaps like Merlin's) has backfired upon her, and as hoodwinked dreamer she now gets her reward in coming to face reality a little too late. The rose cannot shut, and be a bud again.

IV

Whether *The Eve of St. Agnes* is a good poem depends in large part on the reader's willingness to find in it a consistency and unity that may not in fact be there.[13] But however it is evaluated, it stands significantly at

[12] *Hamlet,* IV. 176-179. This point is made by Stuart M. Sperry, "Madeline and Ophelia," *N&Q,* n. s., IV (1957), 29 f.

[13] Keats's conclusion seems a matter for unending debate. The metaphysical critics, remarking that the storm is "an elfin-storm from faery land" and that the lovers "glide, like phantoms" out of the castle, uniformly agree that Madeline and Porphyro transcend mortality, entering an otherworld of eternal felicity, while Angela, the Beadsman, and the warriors remain to die or writhe benightmared. But the "elfin-storm" is Porphyro's explanation; the narrator calls it "a tempest fell" of "frost-wind" and "sharp sleet," and other critics (e.g., Amy Lowell, *John Keats,* Boston, 1925, II, 175; Herbert

the beginning of Keats's single great creative year, 1819, and it serves to introduce a preoccupation of all the major poems of this year: that an individual ought not to lose touch with the realities of this world.

In the poems of 1819, Keats's most explicit, unequivocal statement about the conditions of human life comes in the *Ode on Melancholy*. Life in the world, we are told in the third stanza, is an affair in which pleasure and pain are inseparably mixed. Beauty and the melancholy awareness that beauty must die, joy and the simultaneous fading of joy, "aching Pleasure" and its instant turning to poison—all are inextricably bound up in life. There is no pleasure without pain, and, conversely, if pain is sealed off, so also is pleasure. One accepts the inseparability of pleasure and pain, or one rejects life entirely, and suffers a kind of moral and spiritual emptiness amounting to death. The former is the better alternative: he lives most fully "whose strenuous tongue / Can burst Joy's grape against his palate fine."

The first stanza of the ode contains a series of negatives—what not to do "when the melancholy fit shall fall." Beginning with forgetfulness, progressing through narcotics to poisons and death, the images all represent anodynes to escape pain in life. But they are rejected, because they shut out pleasure as well as pain, and reduce life to nothing: "For shade to shade will come too drowsily, / And drown the wakeful anguish of the soul." Elsewhere in Keats the anodyne is dreaming, trusting in the visionary imagination, and, to cut short further explanation, the dreamer in the poems of 1819 is always one who would escape pain, but hopes, wrongly, to achieve pleasure. Either he comes to grief through his delusion, or he learns his lesson and wakes up.

G. Wright, "Has Keats's 'Eve of St Agnes' a Tragic Ending?," *MLR*, XL, 1945, 90-94; Bernice Slote, *Keats and the Dramatic Principle*, Lincoln, Neb., 1958, pp. 35 f.) have suggested that the lovers face reality, perhaps even perish, in the storm. Still another view (Wright, p. 92) is that the lovers face penance in "that second circle of sad hell," the circle of carnal sinners in the Fifth Canto of the *Inferno*, in which (as Keats described it in his sonnet "On a Dream") lovers are buffeted about in a storm very much like the one in "The Eve of St. Agnes." It is possible that Porphyro is evil only to the extent that Madeline is a hoodwinked dreamer, that when she awakens from her dream the evil represented by him is correspondingly reduced, and a happy human conclusion is justified. But it seems doubtful, and one may at this point have to fall back on the remark of the publisher J. A. Hessey, "[Keats] is such a man of fits and starts he is not much to be depended on" (Edmund Blunden, *Keats's Publisher*, London, 1936, p. 56), or that of Haydon, "never for two days did he know his own intentions" (*The Diary of Benjamin Robert Haydon*, ed. Willard B. Pope, Cambridge, Mass., 1960, II, 317). Whatever the fate of the lovers, Woodhouse noted that Keats "altered the last 3 lines to leave on the reader a sense of pettish disgust. . . . He says he likes that the poem should leave off with this Change of Sentiment" *Letters*, II, 162 f).

Take Madeline as the first instance. In bed, under the delusion that she can achieve bliss in her dream, yet wake up in the virgin morn no weeping Magdalen, she is "Blissfully haven'd both from joy and pain" (240)—for all practical purposes in the narcotic state rejected by the *Ode on Melancholy,* experiencing nothing. Keats reiterates the idea two lines later, "Blinded alike from sunshine and from rain," and the folly of her delusion is represented by the reversal of natural process, "As though a rose should shut, and be a bud again" (242 f.). As generally in Keats's poems, dreaming is attended by fairy-tale imagery: under the spell of "faery fancy," Madeline plays the conjuror, and Porphyro is linked in several ways with fairy-lore, witchcraft, and sorcery, as well as pagan sensuality. It is possible that Madeline never completely awakens from her fanciful dream; for she believes Porphyro when he tells her that the storm is "an elfin-storm from faery land" (343), and she imagines "sleeping dragons all around" (353) when they hurry out of the castle.

The heroine of *The Eve of Saint Mark,* written a week or so after the completion of *The Eve of St. Agnes,* in some ways resembles Madeline. Among the "thousand things" perplexing Bertha in the volume she pores over are "stars of Heaven, and angels' wings, / Martyrs in a fiery blaze, / Azure saints in silver rays" (29-32). Enwrapped in the legend of St. Mark, "dazed with saintly imag'ries" (56), she ignores the life in the village around her, and cuts herself off from reality—a "poor cheated soul" (69), "lost in dizzy maze" [14] and mocked by her own shadow.

The wretched knight-at-arms in *La Belle Dame Sans Merci* is similarly a hoodwinked dreamer. La Belle Dame is "a faery's child"; she sings "A faery's song," speaks "in language strange," and takes him to an "elfin grot." When he awakens from his vision he finds himself "On the cold hill's side." But he is still the dupe of his dream, still hoodwinked, because he continues, in a barren landscape, "Alone and palely loitering," hoping for a second meeting with La Belle Dame. And he denies himself participation in the actual world, which, against his bleak surroundings, is represented as a more fruitful scene, where "The squirrel's granary is full, / And the harvest's done." [15]

[14] A variant following line 68 (Garrod, p. 451 n.). With Walter E. Houghton's interpretation, "The Meaning of Keats's *Eve of St. Mark,*" *ELH*, XIII (1946), 64-78, I disagree in only one point: that Bertha is a "poor cheated soul" not because she is tied down to the actual, wasting away in oblivion, but because she is cheated by her fancy into denying the actual.

[15] In my brief treatment of "La Belle Dame" and "Lamia," as in this section of my paper generally, I am indebted to David Perkins's chapters on Keats in *The Quest for Permanence* (Cambridge, Mass., 1959).

In *Lamia,* the hoodwinked dreamer is of course Lycius, who falls in love with the serpent woman Lamia, in whose veins runs "elfin blood," who lingers by the wayside "fairily," with whom he lives in "sweet sin" in a magical palace with a "faery-roof" (I. 147, 200, II. 31, 123). "She seem'd, at once, some penanced lady elf, / Some demon's mistress, or the demon's self" (I. 55 f.). What she promises to do for Lycius is what, according to the *Ode on Melancholy,* cannot be done for mortal men: "To unperplex bliss from its neighbour pain; / Define their pettish limits, and estrange / Their points of contact, and swift counterchange." The inseparability of pleasure and pain is for her a "specious chaos"; she will separate them "with sure art" (I. 192-196)—or so the blinded Lycius thinks. But "Spells are but made to break," wrote Keats, in a passage subsequently omitted from the text. "A thrill / Of trumpets" reminds Lycius of the claims of the "noisy world almost forsworn" (II. 27-33), and he holds a wedding feast, at which "cold philosophy," in the form of his old tutor Apollonius, attends to put "all charms" to flight. The "foul dream" Lamia vanishes under the tutor's piercing gaze, and Lycius, too engrossed in his dream to survive, falls dead.

From *Lamia,* we may merely dip ino *The Fall of Hyperion* to recall Keats's condemnation of dreamers. They are "vision'ries," "dreamers weak," who seek out wonders, but ignore what is most important, the human face (I. 161-163). "Only the dreamer venoms all his days" (I. 175), the speaker learns on the steps of Moneta's temple. "The poet and the dreamer are distinct, / Diverse, sheer opposite, antipodes. / The one pours out a balm upon the world, / The other vexes it" (I. 199-202).

Keats's mature view of dreamers illuminates perhaps most importantly the two best odes, on a Grecian Urn and to a Nightingale. In each poem the speaker begins as dreamer, hoodwinked with the idea that he can unperplex bliss from its neighbor pain, that he can find an anodyne to the ills of the flesh by joining the timeless life pictured on an urn, or by fading away into the forest with a bird. In each case the result is an awareness that spells are but made to break: the speaker recognizes the falseness of the dream, the shortcomings of the ideal he has created, and he returns to the mortal world. Life on the urn is at first attractive: unheard melodies are sweeter; the lovers will remain young and fair; the trees will never lose their leaves. Yet it is a static situation, in which life is frozen to a standstill, and there is no fulfillment. Love must be enjoyed, not be stopped forever at a point when enjoyment is just out of reach. The final judgment is that the urn is a "Cold Pastoral," a "friend to man" that, as a work of art, teases him out of thought but offers no possible substitute for life in the actual world.

In the *Ode to a Nightingale,* the speaker would fade away with the bird, and forget "The weariness, the fever, and the fret" of the mortal world, "Where Beauty cannot keep her lustrous eyes, / Or new Love pine at them beyond to-morrow." But when he imaginatively joins the bird in the forest, he immediately longs for the world he has just rejected: "Here there is no light. . . . I cannot see what flowers are at my feet." "In embalmed darkness" he is forced to "guess each sweet" of the transient natural world. As he continues musing, the bird takes on for him the fairy-tale associations that we saw earlier connected with Madeline's dream, La Belle Dame, and Lamia: its immortal voice has charmed "magic casements . . . in faery lands forlorn." The realization that the faery lands are forlorn of human life tolls the dreamer back to his sole self, and he wakes up. The nightingale, symbol of dreams and the visionary imagination, has turned out to be a "deceiving elf." The fancy "cannot cheat so well."

The metaphysical critics are right in asserting Keats's early trust in the imagination. What they sometimes fail to recognize, themselves eager for glimpses of heaven's bourne, and to an extent hoodwinked with their own rather than Keats's metaphysics, is that before Keats wrote more than a handful of poems we would not willingly let die, he in large part changed his mind.[16] Late in January 1818, on sitting down to read *King Lear* once again, he wrote a sonnet bidding goodby to romance: "Let me not wander in a barren dream." A few days later he called it "A terrible division" when the soul is flown upward and the body "earthward press'd." [17] In March he wrote, "It is a flaw / In happiness to see beyond our bourn," and about the same time he recognized that "Four seasons" —not just eternal spring, as the visionary might conjure up—"Four seasons fill the measure of the year." Similarly "There are four seasons in the mind of man," who "has his Winter too of pale misfeature, / Or else he would forego his mortal nature." [18] In July, on his walking trip to Scotland, he wrote:

[16] Glen O. Allen, "The Fall of Endymion: A Study in Keats's Intellectual Growth," *K-SJ,* VI (1957), 37-57, argues authoritatively that the change occurred during the winter of 1817-18, while Keats was completing and revising *Endymion.* Ford, p. 141, acknowledges the change, but connects it with *La Belle Dame,* and thereafter discusses among important poems only *Lamia.* Perkins, p. 220, feels that "the over-all course of . . . [Keats's] development might be partly described as a periodic, though gradually cumulative, loss of confidence in the merely visionary imagination."

[17] "God of the Meridian."

[18] "To J. H. Reynolds, Esq.," ll. 82 f.; "Four Seasons."

> Scanty the hour and few the steps beyond the bourn of care,
> Beyond the sweet and bitter world,—beyond it unaware!
> Scanty the hour and few the steps, because a longer stay
> Would bar return, and make a man forget his mortal way:
> O horrible! to lose the sight of well remember'd face. . . .
> No, no, that horror cannot be, for at the cable's length
> Man feels the gentle anchor pull and gladdens in its strength.[19]

It is the gentle anchor of mortality that ties us to the world; man gladdens in its strength. "Fancy," said Keats to Reynolds, "is indeed less than a present palpable reality." It would be a distortion of fact to maintain that he always held this later view, but it is worth noting that even when he and his fancy could not agree, he declared himself "more at home amongst Men and women," happier reading Chaucer than Ariosto.[20]

The dreamer in Keats is ultimately one who turns his back, not merely on the pains of life, but on life altogether; and in the poems of 1819, beginning with *The Eve of St. Agnes,* his dreaming is condemned. If the major concern in these poems is the conflict between actuality and the ideal, the result is not a rejection of the actual, but rather a facing-up to it that amounts, in the total view, to affirmation. It is a notable part of Keats's wisdom that he never lost touch with reality, that he condemned his hoodwinked dreamers who would shut out the world, that he recognized life as a complexity of pleasure and pain, and laid down a rule for action: achievement of the ripest, fullest experience that one is capable of. These qualities make him a saner if in some ways less romantic poet than his contemporaries, and they should qualify him as the Romantic poet most likely to survive in the modern world.

[19] "Lines Written in the Highlands after a Visit to Burns's Country," ll. 29-33, 39 f.
[20] *Letters,* I, 325, II, 234.

The *Ode to Psyche* and the *Ode on Melancholy*

by Harold Bloom

Ode to Psyche

The *Ode to Psyche* has little to do with the accepted myth of Eros and Psyche. That myth is itself scarcely classical; it comes very late, and as an obvious and deliberate allegory. Aphrodite, jealous of the beautiful Psyche who is drawing her admirers away, commands Eros to afflict her with love for a base creature. But he falls in love with her, and comes to her regularly, always in the darkness. When, against his wishes, she lights a candle to see him, he flees from her. She quests for Eros by performing tasks set by Aphrodite, the last of which is a descent into the underworld. Psyche's inquiring spirit, which has previously caused her the loss of her lover, now all but destroys her. Warned by Persephone not to open a box sent by that goddess to Aphrodite, Psyche forsakes control again, and is about to be pulled down forever into the darkness when Eros intervenes, persuades Zeus to make Psyche immortal and to reconcile Aphrodite to her. Restored to each other, the lovers dwell together in Olympus.

Keats begins by bringing the reunited Eros and Psyche down to earth. We do not know whether Keats has seen the lovers in a dream or "with awaken'd eyes" in a vision of reality, but either way he has seen them. He finds them at that moment of Keatsian intensity when they are neither apart nor joined together, but rather in an embrace scarcely ended and another about to commence. Eros he recognizes immediately, but Psyche is revealed to him in a moment of astonished apprehension.

The next two stanzas are parallel in structure, and are deliberately contrary to each other in emphasis and meaning. In the first the machinery of worship—altar, choir, voice, lute, pipe, incense, shrine, grove, oracle, and "heat of pale-mouth'd prophet dreaming"—is subtly deprecated. In the second, though the wording is almost identical, the same apparatus is humanized and eulogized. Keats said ironically that he was "more orthodox" in the old Olympian religion than the ancients, too orthodox "to let a heathen Goddess be so neglected." This heathen Goddess is the human-soul-in-love, which can well dispense with the outward worship ironically regretted in the second stanza, but which deserves and needs the inner worship of the imagination that is offered to it in the third stanza.

The changes of wording between the stanzas are so slight that a careless reading may overlook them. In the first, the Olympian hierarchy is "faded," and Psyche is the loveliest of the gods still evident. The other surviving Olympians are Phoebe and Aphrodite, and they live only in the light of the moon and the evening star. They were worshiped by the ancients; Psyche was not, but she is now fairer than either of them:

> though temple thou hast none.
> Nor altar heap'd with flowers;
> Nor virgin-choir to make delicious moan
> Upon the midnight hours;
> No voice, no lute, no pipe, no incense sweet
> From chain-swung censer teeming;
> No shrine, no grove, no oracle, no heat
> Of pale-mouth'd prophet dreaming.

As the catalog piles up, it is deliberately made to seem a little ludicrous, and the thrust (in context) is against the outer ceremonial of organized religion itself, not just against the Olympian worship. The choir is of virgins, and they make "delicious moan" at midnight: a sly hint of the sexual sublimation in aspects of worship. Then comes the long list of negative properties, whose absence makes them seem faintly ridiculous, until at the incantatory climax the celebrant prophet is evoked, with his heat of possession, his "pale-mouth'd" dreaming, as he longs for Phoebe or Aphrodite. The element of sexual suppression is again subtly conveyed.

When Keats turns to the positive, he employs similar phrases with a different emphasis. First comes a very forceful transition in which the sanctified elements are replaced by the poet finding his inspiration in his own perception of the elements:

> O brightest! though too late for antique vows,
> Too, too late for the fond believing lyre,
> When holy were the haunted forest boughs,
> Holy the air, the water, and the fire;
> Yet even in these days so far retir'd
> From happy pieties, thy lucent fans,
> Fluttering among the faint Olympians,
> I see, and sing, by my own eyes inspir'd.

Too late for antique vows, but in good time for the imaginative vow that Keats is about to give. On one level Keats is still voicing an ostensible regret for the days not "so far retir'd / From happy pieties" (happy in contrast to later pieties), when earth and its forest growths and the other elements were all accounted holy. Now they are not, for other pieties and the analytical mind combine to take away their sanctification. Yet even in these days Keats can *see* one movement, one light, fluttering among the faint Olympians, and because he can see her he can sing, inspired by his own eyes. Atoms of perception become intelligences, as Keats once remarked, because they *see,* they know, and therefore they are god. Seeing Psyche, he knows her, and moves to a union with her in which he becomes a god, a movement of incarnation. The poet is born in his own mind as he moves to become a priest of Psyche, and as a priest he participates in a humanistic and naturalistic communion, an act of the imagination which is a kind of natural supernaturalism. In the passage ending the third stanza the change from "no voice" and "no lute" to "thy voice" and "thy lute" utterly transforms the same phrasing employed earlier:

> So let me be thy choir, and make a moan
> Upon the midnight hours;
> Thy voice, thy lute, thy pipe, thy incense sweet
> From swinged censer teeming;
> Thy shrine, thy grove, thy oracle, thy heat
> Of pale-mouth'd prophet dreaming.

The entire paraphernalia of worship is transformed in this internalization. Not only is Keats himself substituted for the deliciously moaning virgin choir, but Keats's poem, the *Ode to Psyche,* which he is in the act of composing, becomes the "moan upon the midnight hours." The voice, the lute, and the pipe become emblems of the poem that features them. The sweet incense rises from the poem itself, now identified as a "swinged censer teeming," and identified also with Keats himself. The particular change in wording here is revelatory—from "chain-swung censer" to "swinged censer," with the mechanical element omitted. The shrine becomes the fane that Keats will build in his own mind; the grove, the visionary foliage that will rise there as "branched thoughts." The oracle or prophet will be Keats in his role of the figure of the youth as virile poet, the youth of the poet's paradise in Collins and Coleridge, the questing poet shepherd in a state of innocence. The final transformation comes in a triumph of contextualization, as no word needs to be changed in "thy heat / Of pale-mouth'd prophet dreaming." This is not the frustration felt by the aspirant for Phoebe or Aphrodite, because it is *thy* heat, Psyche's, and so Keats and Psyche share it. If it is a reciprocal heat, then the "pale-mouth'd prophet" is at least dreaming of reality.

So far Keats has reached a point parallel to Collins's most imaginative moment in the *Ode on the Poetical Character,* for Keats has identified himself as a prophet of the loving human soul, and is poised before declaring that the paradise for the soul is to be built by the poet's imagination within the poet's own consciousness. In the final stanza Keats goes beyond Collins, with the general influence of Wordsworth determining the extent of that advance:

> Yes, I will be thy priest, and build a fane
>   In some untrodden region of my mind,
> Where branched thoughts, new grown with pleasant pain,
>   Instead of pines shall murmur in the wind

Collins wrote in the light of Milton; Keats in the more inward-shining light of Wordsworth. In the lines from *The Recluse,* prefacing *The Excursion,* Keats had read Wordsworth's invocation of a greater Muse than Milton's:

>   if such
> Descend to earth or dwell in highest heaven!
> For I must tread on shadowy ground

That "shadowy ground" is the haunt of Keats's "shadowy thought," and its place is "the Mind of Man," which Wordsworth calls "the main region of my song." Wordsworth seeks his "groves Elysian" in a wedding between "the discerning intellect of Man" and "his goodly universe" of nature. Keats, in the last stanza of *To Psyche,* finds the goodly universe to be produced within the discerning intellect by the agency of poetry.

The opening lines of this stanza state that Psyche's temple will be built "in some untrodden region" of Keats's mind. The implication is that the process is one of soul-making in an undiscovered country; to build Psyche's temple is to widen consciousness. But an increase in consciousness carries with it the dual capacity for pleasure or for pain. The thoughts that will grow like branches in that heretofore untrodden region will be grown "with pleasant pain"; the oxymoron, Keats's most characteristic rhetorical device, is peculiarly appropriate to any rendition of an earthly or poet's paradise, a Beulah land where, as Blake said, all contrary statements are equally true.

The branched thoughts, in this inner nature, replace pines, and murmur in the wind of inspiration.

> Far, far around shall those dark-cluster'd trees
> Fledge the wild-ridged mountains steep by steep;
> And there by zephyrs, streams, and birds, and bees,
> The moss-lain Dryads shall be lull'd to sleep

It takes an effort to recollect that these mountains and other phenomena are all within the mind. The pastoral landscape is completed by the Dryads, who can no longer be lulled to sleep in the external woods now "retir'd from happy pieties" but who find their repose in this mental paradise. Having created a more ideal nature, Keats proceeds to embower within it a sanctuary for Psyche:

> And in the midst of this wide quietness
> A rosy sanctuary will I dress
> With the wreath'd trellis of a working brain,
> With buds, and bells, and stars without a name,
> With all the gardener Fancy e'er could feign,
> Who breeding flowers, will never breed the same

The "wide quietness" framed by the "wild-ridged mountains," themselves plumed by the "dark-cluster'd trees," reminds us of the Wordsworthian landscape near Tintern Abbey, where the steep and lofty cliffs impressed thoughts of deeper seclusion on an already secluded scene, and connected the landscape with the quiet of the sky. But whereas Wordsworth's scene is a given outward phenomenon, Keats's is built up within. And so he refers to the function of his working brain within his general consciousness as being that of a "wreath'd trellis," a gardener's support for clinging vines. In Keats's most definitive vision of a poet's paradise, at the opening of *The Fall of Hyperion,* this natural emblem appears again:

> . . . and by the touch
> Of scent, not far from roses. Turning round
> I saw an arbour with a drooping roof
> Of trellis vines, and bells, and larger blooms,
> Like floral censers, swinging light in air

It is Psyche's rosy sanctuary, but also the arbor where "our Mother Eve" had her last meal in Paradise, a feast of summer fruits. In the *Ode* the sanctuary is dressed not only with buds and bells but with "stars without a name," for here the unrestricted invention of the Fancy is at work. But Paradise was lost, and the Paradise of the poet's fancy has an ambiguous and fragile nature. What follows is the triumph of Keats's *Ode,* and the most complex effect in it: the somber but defiant acknowledgment of invention's limits, and the closing declaration of the human love that surmounts even imaginative limitations. Where Collins's *Ode* ends in a grim acknowledgment that the time cannot be imaginatively redeemed, at least not by himself, Keats chooses to end with an image of an open casement, through which the warm Love, Psyche's Eros, shall yet enter.

Keats prepares his poem's rhapsodical climax by coming to a full but open stop after a couplet that rivals any as an epitome of the myth-making faculty:

> With all the gardener Fancy e'er could feign,
> Who breeding flowers, will never breed the same

Keats, in his use of "feign" in this context, may be recalling the critic Touchstone in *As You Like It.* Audrey says: "I do not know what poetical is. Is it honest in deed and word? Is it a true thing?" Touchstone replies: "No, truly; for the truest poetry is the most feigning." Keats's rich word "feign," with its mingled dignity and ruin, is parallel to the word "artifice" in Yeats's myth of poetic self-recognition in *Sailing to Byzantium.* Yeats appeals to the beings who stand in the holy fire of the state

Blake called Eden, where the creator and the creation are one. It is a fire that can be walked through; it will not singe a sleeve. Yet it can consume the natural heart away. This is Yeats's prayer to his masters in the fire, who would include Blake and Shelley and Keats: consume away what is sick with desire and yet cannot know itself, for it is fastened to dying, to the contrary to desire. And, having done this, gather me into the *artifice* of eternity. The gardener Fancy only feigns, and when he makes his artifice, breeds his flower, he cannot make or breed the same again, as a natural gardener could. But the orders of reality contend here; the natural gardener breeds only in finite variety, but the abundance of the imagination is endless, and each imaginative breeding is unique.

The poem *Ode to Psyche* is unique, and also central, for its art is a natural growth out of nature, based as it is upon a very particular act of consciousness, which Keats arrests in all its concreteness. Keats's real parallel among the myth-makers is Wallace Stevens, as Collins's is Coleridge, and Blake's is, more or less, Yeats. Keats's Psyche is a sexual goddess who renews consciousness and thus renews the earth, and for Stevens as for Keats the earth is enough. The ode *To Autumn* finds its companion in Wallace Stevens's *Sunday Morning,* and *To Psyche* is closely related to some of the *Credences of Summer.* Stevens writes of seeing nature as "the very thing and nothing else," and "without evasion by a single metaphor." Keats grows a foliage within his mind so as to have a natural shrine for Psyche which shall be eternal. Stevens says, take the phenomenon of nature and:

> Look at it in its essential barrenness
> And say this, this is the centre that I seek.
> Fix it in an eternal foliage
>
> And fill the foliage with arrested peace,
> Joy of such permanence, right ignorance
> Of change still possible. Exile desire
> For what is not. This is the barrenness
> Of the fertile thing that can attain no more.

The gardener Fancy, breeding flowers, will never breed the same, for his feigning gives us that same barrenness, the barrenness of the fertile thing that can attain no more, a fixed perfection that lacks both the flaw and the virtue of green life. This paradox is more overt in the *Ode on a Grecian Urn* and in *Byzantium,* where the glory of changeless metal can scorn common bird or petal, and yet must be embittered by the changing and sexually governing moon. What unites Keats and Stevens is a temper of naturalistic acceptance, without bitterness or protest, of the paradox of the Romantic Imagination. Keats carries the honesty of acceptance to the point where it is impossible to judge whether the flaw or virtue of the gardener Fancy is offered to Psyche as the poet's best gift. "*With all* the gardener Fancy e'er could feign," he says. The final offer is Keats's human absolute; he does not offer Psyche the truth of the Imagination, for he is uncertain of the kind of truth involved, but gives her instead the holiness of the heart's affections:

> And there shall be for thee all soft delight
> That shadowy thought can win,
> A bright torch, and a casement ope at night,
> To let the warm Love in!

There is a play, in these final lines, upon the familiar myth of Eros and Psyche which Keats has put aside in the main body of his ode. The mythical love of Eros and Psyche was an act in darkness; the bright torch burns in the natural tower of consciousness which Keats has built for the lovers' shrine. The open casement may remind us of the magic casements that open on the faery vision of the *Nightingale* ode, in the fading of the song of that more ambitious poem. Here, in *To Psyche,* it emphasizes the openness of the imagination toward the heart's affections. The subtle genius of Keats shades his ode even at its exultant surrender; there shall be for the soul "all soft delight / That *shadowy* thought can win." Thought is foliage here, and the green shade will shelter the soul, but the green thought itself is shadowy, which again suggests its limitations. Like the other great Romantics, Keats distrusted the Beulah of earthly repose, the natural garden of a world that he longed for. And, like his major contemporaries, he went on from it to a myth that promised a humanism that could transcend Nature's illusions.

Ode on Melancholy

The difficulties of the *Ode on Melancholy* are infrequently realized because the poem is not often closely read. Yet even a superficial reading involves us in Keats's deliberately unresolved contraries. The admonition of the first stanza is against false melancholy, courted for the sake of the supposed oblivion it brings. But oblivion is not to be hired; for Keats true melancholy involves a sudden increase in consciousness, not a gradual evasion of its claims.

Keats canceled the initial opening stanza of this ode presumably because he saw that the poem's harmony was threatened if fully half of it were concerned with the useless quest after "the Melancholy." His sense of proportion did not fail him in this, and yet something went out of the poem with the exclusion of that stanza:

> Though you should build a bark of dead men's bones,
> And rear a phantom gibbet for a mast,
> Stitch shrouds together for a sail, with groans
> To fill it out, blood-stained and aghast;
> Although your rudder be a dragon's tail
> Long sever'd, yet still hard with agony,
> Your cordage large uprootings from the skull
> Of bald Medusa, certes you would fail
> To find the Melancholy—whether she
> Dreameth in any isle of Lethe dull.

The "whether" in the ninth line may be read as "even if." This remarkable and grisly stanza is more than the reverse of an invitation to the voyage. Its irony is palpable; its humor is in the enormous labor of Gothicizing despair which is necessarily in vain, for the mythic beast, Melancholy, cannot thus be confronted. The tone of the stanza changes with the dash in line 9; with it the voice speaking the poem ceases to be ironical. With the next stanza, the first of the received text, the voice is passionate, though its message is the same. By excluding the original first stanza, Keats lost a grim humor that finds only a thin echo at the poem's close. That humor, in juxtaposition to the poem's intensities, would have been parallel to successful clowning in a tragedy.

As the poem stands, the idle quest after the Melancholy is yet inviting:

> No, no, go not to Lethe, neither twist
> Wolf's-bane, tight-rooted, for its poisonous wine;
> Nor suffer thy pale forehead to be kiss'd
> By nightshade, ruby grape of Proserpine;
> Make not your rosary of yew-berries,
> Nor let the beetle, nor the death-moth be
> Your mournful Psyche, nor the downy owl
> A partner in your sorrow's mysteries;
> For shade to shade will come too drowsily,
> And drown the wakeful anguish of the soul.

What is most important here is "*too* drowsily" and "*wakeful* anguish." The truest parallel is in the first stanza of the *Ode to a Nightingale.* There the drowsiness is not excessive; it numbs, but the soul's anguish remains wakeful. The properties of questing after the Melancholy are there also; hemlock, a dull opiate, Lethe, but only in the form of "as though." The melancholy is genuine there, as it is here. It is as though Keats had quested after the epiphanies of these poems, but he has not. The negative grace of the state of being these odes embody falls suddenly, comes with the sharp immediacy of a blow. "My heart aches"; the three heavily accented syllables begin the poem by battering three times at the poet's and our consciousness. "But when the melancholy fit shall fall / Sudden from heaven . . ." is the equivalent in this ode. But when it falls without one's having provoked it, "Then glut thy sorrow"; one need show no restraint in feeding it further. On what? The melancholy fit has fallen as the rains of April fall, to "foster the droop-headed flowers," to cover the hills with green. The shock is that this green fostering, for all its beauty, *is* like the fall of melancholy, for April's green is here called "an April shroud." The enduring color of fresh life is only a grave color, and so your sorrow can also be glutted on the loveliness of such supposedly non-sorrowful emblems as a morning rose, a shore rainbow, or the wealth of globed peonies. To complete the complexity, Keats offers as food for sorrow the *wealth* of one's beloved's "rich anger."

The force of this second stanza is that it is inexplicable, unresolved, until it is suddenly clarified by the first line of the final stanza:

> She dwells with Beauty—Beauty that must die

The line relies on its immediate expository force after the puzzle of the preceding stanza; it requires a long pause after reading. The emphasis needs to be put upon "*must* die"; the anger of the mistress, which so delights the sadism-hunting scholar, is significant only in its richness, not in any sexual implication. It is rich because it offers a possibility of feeding deeply upon an animated beauty that is doomed to lose all motion, all force. Animation, as in its root meaning, here reveals the living soul in full activity, with the special poignance that in this poem is definitive of true melancholy, consciousness of mutability and death. Like Wallace Stevens in *Sunday Morning, Esthétique du Mal* (especially Section XV, the poem's conclusion), and *The Rock,* Keats is insisting on the mingled heroic ethic and humanist aesthetic that the natural is beautiful and apocalyptic precisely because it is physical and ephemeral. Keats's contrast is in his tense insistence that *something* in nature *must* prevail, and his final despair that nothing can, even as the parallel and contrast to Stevens is Yeats, in his insistence (however ironic) that Byzantine realities are superior to mere natural beauties. Spenser in the *Mutabilitie* Cantos and Milton throughout his work resolve these conflicts by a cosmic dialectic. It remained for Blake and Wordsworth, in their very different ways, to humanize these resolutions. With younger and modern Romantics it has been too late in the day to offer full measure in these conflicts; bitterness, however visionary, necessarily keeps breaking in.

The magnificence of the *Ode on Melancholy*'s final stanza is in its exactness of diction as it defines the harmony of continued apprehension of its unresolved contraries. Only Beauty that *must* die is beauty; Joy cannot be present without simultaneously bidding adieu: and *aching* Pleasure (the adjective triumphantly embodies a pair of contraries) is immanent only by turning to poison for us, even as we sip its real (not supposed) honey. For, like the rest of Keats's odes, this poem is tragic, it reaches beyond the disillusionments of a state of experience into the farther innocence of a poet's paradise, as in the shrine of Moneta in the *Fall of Hyperion,* to which this is surely a reference (the "has" helps establish it):

> Ay, in the very temple of delight
> Veil'd Melancholy has her sovran shrine

And, as in *The Fall of Hyperion,* this truth is seen by none except those who earn the poet's melancholy, which is not to be usurped. The *strenuous* tongue does not simply sip the grape's juice; it *bursts* the grape of Joy, with the inevitable double consequence of tasting might and the sadness of might, Moneta's or the Melancholy's double aspect, the Goddess as Muse and as Destroyer:

> And be among her cloudy trophies hung.

The *Ode to a Nightingale*

by David Perkins

. . . The problem, then, is how, with such a temperament, to achieve a spacious lyric expression. It is resolved in the *Ode on a Grecian Urn* and *Ode to a Nightingale,* as in many of the sonnets, by focusing on a particular object and staying with it—in other words, by use of a central symbol. If this is something of a technical innovation within the genre of the ode (though at times Shelley does a rather similar thing), it is, like most such innovations, accomplished not for the sake of mere novelty, but as a means of surmounting a personal dilemma. But the symbol does not dissolve the uncertainty, the openness to many points of view, which made necessary the resort to it. Instead it merely permits the lyric to be written by providing a field within which contrary attitudes may engage and seek a resolution.

Although the *Ode to a Nightingale* ranges more widely than the *Ode on a Grecian Urn,* the poem can also be regarded as the exploration or testing out of a symbol, and, compared with the urn as a symbol, the nightingale would seem to have both limitations and advantages. The advantage of the urn is that it does convey the notion of experience immortally prolonged, but it does not readily allow the poet to enter and share the life it portrays. He has to stand on the outside as a spectator. The nightingale, however, has a living identity and sings to the senses, thus allowing a massive sympathetic response. The liability is that unlike the urn the song of the nightingale does not suggest something potentially eternal. It is true that in his ardor the poet momentarily makes it immortal, but he does so at the cost of destroying any sympathetic union with it, and, in the logic of the poem, virtually compels it to fly away. Hence the same sympathetic grip that makes the experience vivid to the

"The *Ode to a Nightingale.*" From *The Quest for Permanence: The Symbolism of Wordsworth, Shelley, and Keats* (Cambridge, Mass.: Harvard University Press, 1959) by David Perkins.

point that one would wish to prolong it, also forces the recognition that it must be short-lived.

The dramatic development that takes place in the ode lies partly in the gradual transformation of a living nightingale into a symbol of visionary art. By means of the symbol the ode explores the consequences of a commitment to vision, and as it does so, comes close to implying that the destruction of the protagonist is one of the results. In the verse previous to the odes, Keats had occasionally associated creative activity—whether visionary or not—with death. There is nothing surprising in this. Many artists have expressed themselves in a similar way; notions of withdrawal and self-immolation are all too readily suggested by creative enterprise. The distinction is partly that Keats makes poetry of the theme, and partly that he gives it an individual bias. In *Sleep and Poetry* there is the representative remark that in "the o'erwhelming sweets" of poetry he might "die a death/ Of luxury" (lines 58-59), and in a passage from *Endymion* which clearly anticipates the *Ode to a Nightingale,* the shepherds were

> Such as sat listening round Apollo's pipe,
> When the great deity, for earth too ripe,
> Let his divinity o'erflowing die
> In music. (I,141-144)

Here Apollo reveals his divinity by letting it die. Similarly, the nightingale "pouring forth" its "soul abroad" is both declaring its identity or "soul" and dying. But, of course, the nightingale is not thought to be literally dying. The point is that the deity or the nightingale can sing without dying. But as the ode makes clear, man cannot, or, at least, not in a visionary way.

For Keats progressively tended to connect death with purely visionary excursions—in other words, with fantasy and dreams. We noted that the visionary flight usually begins with a partial loss of consciousness. In the more objective, narrative structure of *Lamia* and *The Fall of Hyperion* the equivalent to this "drowsy numbness" would be the "cloudy swoon" which overcomes both Lycius and the poet in *The Fall of Hyperion.* Thus when Lycius first meets Lamia he believes that she is about to "fade" and beseeches her to stay, saying "Even as thou vanishest so shall I die" (I, 260). But as Lamia still threatens to depart, Lycius swoons. Similarly, in *The Fall of Hyperion* the poet drinks of a "transparent juice" which is compared to poison and causes him to lose consciousness:

> No poison gender'd in close monkish cell,
> To thin the scarlet conclave of old men,
> Could so have rapt unwilling life away. (I, 49-51)

In both these poems, then, the swoon which precedes visionary activity is presented as a kind of death, and in *Lamia* it later leads to the actual death of Lycius. In *The Fall of Hyperion* the poet, having entered realms of fantasy, would also have died had he not been able to go through or beyond them by mounting the altar steps and confronting the tragic countenance of Moneta. In the *Ode to a Nightingale* a similar development takes place. It begins with the poet in a state of "drowsy numbness" which, he says, is as though he had taken poison (hemlock) and were dying ("Lethe-wards had sunk"). The further movement of the poet into the nightingale's world also involves a steady movement toward death and a momentary acceptance of it. Then at the beginning of the seventh stanza the nightingale stands revealed for what it is, or rather for what the poet, using it as a symbol, has made of it. No longer a part of the natural world, it is an "immortal Bird" living in a visionary realm. It is almost analogous to La Belle Dame Sans Merci or Lamia luring men to fantasy and death. But, of course, the attitude to the nightingale is quite different from that adopted to Lamia. Keats seems to feel the attraction of what both Lamia and the nightingale represent much more strongly in the ode, and as a result the conflict is not resolved to the extent that it is in the later poem. Or perhaps one should simply say that a different symbol would compel a different attitude.

As the poem opens, the poet hears the nightingale and participates in its life. The happiness he shares is so intense that for the poet it becomes the paradoxically "aching pleasure" of the *Ode on Melancholy,* a pleasure felt as pain ("My heart aches, and a drowsy numbness/ Pains . . ."). But at the same time, this suspense or obliteration of conscious, waking faculties releases the imagination,[1] which is already turning upon the

[1] One can here recall that, in the *Ode on Indolence,* the "Masque-like figures" of Love, Ambition, and Poesy come to wake the poet from a numbing trance:

> The blissful cloud of summer-indolence
> Benumb'd my eyes; my pulse grew less and less;
> Pain had no sting, and pleasure's wreath no flower.

The three figures summon the poet to enterprise in the human world, but they are dismissed, and partly because the trance is favorable to visionary activity: "Farewell! I yet have visions for the night,/ And for the day faint visions there is store."

nightingale and seeing it as something more (or less) than a bird. It is a Dryad from the Arcadian world, like the "moss-lain Dryads" of the *Ode to Psyche.* Its happiness is reiterated, recalling both the "happy, happy boughs" of the urn and also Psyche, the "happy, happy dove." And although the time is mid-May, the nightingale sings of summer, the time of fulfillment. But the nightingale, now singing from a "plot/ Of beechen green," is going to "fade away into the forest dim," and the poet wishes to fade with it. Of this desire the appeal to wine is the first symbolic expression. It is a necessary gesture because the poet in his numbness can scarcely respond to the song, and also because without a further drugging the song is not an unmingled pleasure. . . .

. . . Thus wine was at one time or another explicitly linked with poetry, with imagination, with happiness, with "heaven," in short with all that the nightingale represents. Moreover, in the second stanza, wine resembles the nightingale in being associated with summer, happiness and song—"Provençal song and sun-burnt mirth." Like the "immortal Bird," the wine comes from a "long age," and the reiteration of the word "full," the fullness of the beaker, suggests a desire for an intense, glutted experiencing similar to the poet's deep reaction to the song of the nightingale.

But the impulse to leave the world leads inevitably to a recollection of actual human life. Mortal existence, as the poet thinks of it, has a distorted and ghastly resemblance to his own state of mind in the first stanza. As he hears the nightingale's song, so "men sit and hear each other groan." The poet has been drowsy as though drugged; men are weary. He has been glutted or "too happy" with the song of the nightingale; men are "full of sorrow." [2] In human life "Beauty cannot keep her lustrous eyes,/ Or new Love pine at them beyond to-morrow." There can be no actual prolonging either of what is beautiful in itself or of an intense response to it. Furthermore, except in moments of escape, life inevitably involves pain, for "but to think" (which I take as meaning to be fully conscious rather than in the numbed state favorable to visions) "is to be full of sorrow." At this point, then, the poet is firmly planted in the world of process—"Here." But his wish is still to "fade far away, dissolve, and quite forget," to enter a visionary world of immortal, unmingled bliss, and the wish seems to be reinforced by his recollection of "the weariness, the fever, and the fret" of mortal experience. For the fourth stanza opens by reiterating the will to escape with greater urgency

[2] Wasserman, *The Finer Tone,* p. 208, points out the contrasts between stanzas two and three.

and emotional force—"Away! away! for I will fly to thee." The vehicle of the flight is now no longer wine ("Not charioted by Bacchus and his pards") but Poesy, and in this context Poesy means visionary poetry, or one might even call it fantasy.

Supposing himself to be with the nightingale ("Already with thee!") and associating it with the forest and with darkness, the poet now thinks of a verdurous bower and luxuriously describes it. Like the earlier stanza about wine, the extended imagery of flowers represents a momentary release achieved through the imagination, and, indeed, the capability of the imagination is dramatized in the poetry. In the darkness the poet cannot see the flowers, but precisely for that reason he can see and describe them all the better. The song-haunted darkness stimulates the imagination to "guess each sweet." And the statement that the poet "cannot see . . . what soft incense hangs upon the boughs" is, of course, a typical example of Keats's use of synesthesia, but it is more than that: it is a vivid assertion of the power of the imagination to see more than the sensory eye can see. It converts the incense into something virtually solid so that, as one reads the line, it presents what is very close to a visual image.

One can repeat all this by referring to the over-all metaphoric pattern on which the poem is constructed. The Provençal world suggested by the wine comes as an early anticipation of the realm into which one would wish to retreat. The continuing vehicle of escape is the song of the nightingale; for, as the poet in his trance contemplates the nightingale, he sees it withdrawing further and further from the human world. In stanzas iv through vi, through most of which the poet feels himself to be with the nightingale, the movement is not yet completed, and, as the poem proceeds, the nightingale finally crosses into a realm where the poet cannot follow. But there is a momentary union, and in it the poet, standing in the forest, is able, like the nightingale, to sing of summer even though the time of year is only mid-May. For process is actively taking place within the forest. The violets are "fast fading" and are being replaced by the "coming musk-rose," and as the poet, conscious of the process, thinks of the musk-rose, his imagination leaps ahead to the time of fulfillment and completion when the musk-rose will be "the murmurous haunt of flies on summer eves." Here, of course, under the spell of the nightingale and by means of the imagery of flowers, the poet is able to contemplate process with a serenity anticipating the ode *To Autumn,* but as *To Autumn* makes clear, a strong commitment to process leads to the thought of death and even permits one to acquiesce in it. In this connection, one should note that the darkness is described as "embalmèd." The primary sense of the word in this context is "perfumed," but there is also the suggestion of death, as though to be in the forest were a scented, hushed burial.

Throughout the poem darkness has been gathering about the poet as he moves into the nightingale world—"there is no light"; "I cannot see"; "embalmèd darkness." Now the poet remains in the dark, still hearing the song of the nightingale:

> Darkling I listen; and, for many a time
> I have been half in love with easeful Death,
> Call'd him soft names in many a musèd rhyme,
> To take into the air my quiet breath.

Keats repeatedly used "easeful Death" as an escape symbol. Thus in *Endymion* after listing the ills of life, the hero says that they have "in themselves" a "good": they make us feel "How quiet death is" (II, 159). One might also cite the sonnet, "After dark vapours," where the poet speaks of a moment of release after the oppression of a "long dreary season" of bad weather. At such a time "calmest thoughts come round us," and the sestet goes on to list some of these in a series of images. The progression moves from images of hushed natural process—"Fruit ripening in stillness"—to a hypnotic sense of time running out, and comes to an end with "a Poet's death."

But the release Keats meditated in death was not always conceived as merely quiet and easeful. It can also be "rich to die" in that the poet, groping for a symbol of fulfillment or intensity, thinks of death as a positive experience. The sonnet "Why did I laugh" even anticipates the phrasing of the ode as it concludes:

> Yet would I on this very midnight cease,
> And the world's gaudy ensigns see in shreds;
> Verse, Fame, and Beauty are intense indeed,
> But Death intenser—Death is Life's high meed.

So, in a loose moment, Keats wrote Fanny Brawne, "I have two luxuries to brood over in my walks, your Loveliness and the hour of my death." Nor is it difficult to see how, for Keats, death becomes associated with fulfillment. In the first place, a massive intensity (as Keats envisages this impossible state) turns finally into oblivion—or at least into a suspended animation not unlike death. So Clymene, for example, describes for the assembled Titans in *Hyperion* the music of Apollo:

my sense was fill'd
With that new blissful golden melody.
A living death was in each gush of sounds. (II, 279-281)

Secondly, in the world of process, fulfillment and death are often simultaneous. This perception receives a specifically sexual expression at the end of the "Bright Star" sonnet. Keats apparently had trouble with the last lines,

Still, still to hear her tender-taken breath,
And so live ever—or else swoon to death,

and it is difficult to know how they should be read. They might imply no more than a hyperbole which could be paraphrased, "If I can't have this forever, let me die before it fades." Or the phrase "swoon to death" might specifically refer to a sexual climax which would end the passionate, "sweet unrest." But especially if one takes account of the last line of the original version— "Half-passionless, and so swoon on to death"— the notion would also seem to be that experience so intense must end in numbness and death.

Throughout the ode the poet has been steadily relinquishing a grip on actuality until now, under the influence of the song, it has become possible to assert that death would be a climactic release and outpouring desirable in itself and the more desirable because it would bar a return to the human world "Where Beauty cannot keep her lustrous eyes":

Now more than ever seems it rich to die,
To cease upon the midnight with no pain,
While thou art pouring forth thy soul abroad
In such an ecstasy!

But if death represents a form of escape more final and complete than wine or Poesy, it does not suggest a further union with the nightingale, or a prolongation of hearing its song:

Still wouldst thou sing, and I have ears in vain—
To thy high requiem become a sod.

"Land and Sea, weakness and decline," Keats once wrote, "are great separators, but death is the great divorcer for ever." The final lines of the stanza represent the speaker's sudden recollection of this fact and a return to actuality compelled by recognizing the direction in which he has been moving.

By the end of the sixth stanza, then, the human and nightingale worlds have been entirely sundered. At once the poet turns directly to the nightingale in a passionate apostrophe: "Thou wast not born for death." To the objection so often raised, that this particular bird will die, one can only reply that in its distance from the poet the nightingale has now been openly transformed into symbol. Indeed, the poem now largely parallels the last stanza of the *Ode on a Grecian Urn*. Like the urn, which is compared to eternity, the bird is immortal, and its life is contrasted with the "passing night" or brief generations of man. Here, of course, Keats employs a brilliant poetic tact to justify the symbolic assertion. By referring only to the voice of the nightingale, he can identify it with all nightingales and so find a natural basis for claiming that, like the urn, it has remained "in midst of other woe/ Than ours, a friend to man." It has been heard by all men—"emperor and clown" (or rustic)—and "perhaps" its song "found a path/ Through the sad heart of Ruth."

But throughout the seventh stanza the nightingale, even as a symbol, continues to move farther away from the human world. It is heard first by "emperor and clown" figures presumably out of the historical past, then by Ruth in a world of Biblical legend, and finally it is heard in "faery lands," and these faery lands may be the faery lands or "elfin grot" of *La Belle Dame Sans Merci*—a place which may represent a destructive illusion. The faery lands are "forlorn" because man cannot live in them. For the same reason the song of the nightingale is no longer happy. Instead it is a "requiem" or "plaintive anthem." And as the poet awakens from his trance, there is even the suggestion that the visions stimulated by the song of the nightingale may have been illusory; for the poet, bidding farewell to the vision, says

> Adieu! the fancy cannot cheat so well
> As she is fam'd to do, deceiving elf.

Finally, one may note that it is not the bird that "fades" but its song, and this does not happen until the poet has been tolled back to his "sole self." Thus if the departure represents the flight of a living bird, it is also presented as the fading of a vision. Moreover, the song does not merely fade. With a final, ironic reflection upon the theme of death, it is described as "buried," as if to imply the denial of any possibility of hearing it. And the poem ends with uncertainty and a question: was the process that has taken place a momentary glimpse of truth (a "vision"), or a musing subjective half-dream; and is the poet's inability to experience it now an awakening into reality or a lapse into insensibility:

> Was it a vision, or a waking dream?
> Fled is that music:—Do I wake or sleep?

The question is one that has haunted poetry ever since the romantic age, and poets, writing their own versions of Keats's great ode, have often used virtually an identical symbol. . . .

The *Ode on a Grecian Urn*

by Earl Wasserman

I

Let us first assume the loosest possible framework for the poem and then observe the way in which the actions of the images qualify and orient the general meaning. No one will deny that the ode, like most of Keats's poems, deals with the human and mutable on the one hand, and the immortal and essential on the other; and that what it states has something to do with both an opposition and a fusion of these two states. On this note the poem opens, for the poet softly addresses the urn as a "still unravish'd bride."

Now, such tender reverence for what normally is an undesirable condition—to say nothing of the startling force of the word "unravish'd" as applied to "bride"—calls for some inquiry. Between the realm of the merely human, where passion leaves "a heart high-sorrowful and cloy'd," and the immortal, where "Real are the dreams of Gods,"[1] there is in Keats's cosmology the knife-edge where the two meet and are indistinguishably present. On the shores of darkness, Keats wrote, "there is light,/ And precipices show untrodden green; / There is a budding morrow in midnight."[2] To Homer, the prototype of the poet, he added, such imaginative insight was granted that, although physically blind, he could penetrate into the nature of things so as to perceive, beyond their outward forms, the essence of light, which contains both light and darkness, and

"The *Ode on a Grecian Urn*." From *The Finer Tone: Keats' Major Poems* (Baltimore: The Johns Hopkins University Press, 1953) by Earl Wasserman. The discussion has been considerably shortened by the author especially for the present volume. The line numbers that occasionally appear throughout the text in parentheses refer to line numbers of the poem.

[1] *Lamia,* I. 127.

[2] "To Homer."

the essence of day, which contains both midnight and morning. The power that perceives this paradoxical essence is an equally paradoxical "blindness keen."

For the expression of this paradoxical essence I shall borrow Kenneth Burke's excellent term "oxymoron" in order to designate not merely the paradoxical collocation of contraries (e.g., freezing heat) but the mystic interfusion of these contraries. To this point of mystic oxymoron and no farther, Keats held, can the human imagination occasionally and momentarily rise as it seeks to overcome the weariness, the fever, and the fret. In *Endymion,* the worshippers of Pan pray that the earth-god

> Be still the unimaginable lodge
> For solitary thinkings; such as dodge
> Conception to the very bourne of heaven,
> Then leave the naked brain: be still the leaven,
> That spreading in this dull and clodded earth
> Gives it a touch ethereal—a new birth:
> Be still a symbol of immensity;
> A firmament reflected in a sea;
> An element filling the space between;
> An unknown—but no more.[3]

Were Pan more, he would be an unknowable, outside man's range, beyond the bourne, and therefore in the realm of pure immortality, which, in Keats's theology, can never be the home of man either in this life or in the next. Instead, Pan is the concurrence of the mortal and immortal, and hence a knowable unknown without being any the less unknown: he invests the physical with the ethereal; he is the perceptible reflection of the imperceptible; his is the oxymoronic nature of heaven's bourne.

Although the ode is a symbolic action in terms of an urn, its intrinsic theme is that region where earth and the ethereal, light and darkness, time and no-time become one; and what the symbolic drama ultimately discovers is the way in which art (the urn) relates man to that region. For the bourne of heaven is the outermost limit of the imagination after it has left naked the materialistic brain, which tries to seize everything in a clear, and therefore merely earthly, conception.

To this area of mystic oxymoron the unravished bride very nearly belongs. On the literal level, the urn has existed in the physical world, in which all things are mutable, and so is related to aspects of time and

[3] *Endymion,* I. 293-302.

sound. And yet, by enduring long, it has not only caused them to become secondary factors in its existence (an unravished *bride,* and a *foster*-child), but has become related to their dimensional negatives: quietness, silence, slow time. It exists amid dimensions, and yet, by resisting their usual destructive effects, is tending to make them irrelevant to its existence. In another sense also it approaches the bourne of heaven, for "bride," suggesting the first phase of the process of generation, has reference to the human and mutable, and consequently has the same paradoxical relation to "unravish'd" that morrow has to midnight: the urn belongs to both becoming and immutability, the fluid and the fixed. But the urn only approaches this region, since the statement that it is *still* unravished carries with it the threat that it eventually may be ravished, and since it is related to slow time rather than to no-time. The deceleration is only moving the urn in the direction of the extra-temporal.

This same hesitantly suggested collocation of the mortal and the immortal, and of the dynamic and the static, makes up the loose fabric of the entire first stanza. The figures on the urn are deities or mortals—or both (6); and the emphasis lies on the last suggestion, especially as Keats repeats his doubt, interchanging the terms to blur their difference: "What men or gods are these?" (8) Mortal and immortal move close to the knife-edge, but Keats's question, although it brings them together in the same context, expresses a hesitation that prevents them from fusing. The same loose mingling appears in the line "In Tempe or the dales of Arcady" (7), Tempe being that earthly region which the gods, especially Apollo, were inclined to favor—an earthly heaven—and Arcady that region that man thought to approach most nearly a paradise—a heavenly earth. In each name both the divine and the mortal are present, but with inverted emphasis.

Moreover, the urn itself embodies both conditions, but only in its two different roles; and thus the opposites become associated but still fail to coalesce. As total urn it is related to silence and slow time; yet the figures on the frieze that the quiet urn contains are characterized by their quick and energetic movements and by their music, made noisy by the explosive-laden words "pipes" and "timbrels." Silence and sound, the timeless and the timeful, are nicely counterpoised by the imagery, the music, and the tempo of the stanza.

Finally, the urn, although a bride, is still unravished; the maidens, although unmarried, are in imminent danger of ravishment. The urn, although it has been for ages in the world of mutable becoming, has been unaffected by the acts that belong to becoming because it is not alive;

mortality is not its vital principle. The maidens, although their chastity relates them to the world of pure and changeless being, seem about to be despoiled this very moment by the generative act that symbolizes the world of becoming; because they are mortal, mutability and decay are their vital principle.

But just as the slightest shift of our glance brings to us now the nearly eternal urn, and now the nearly fleeting movements of the pastoral scene on it, so the two qualities, stasis and flux, are not sharply juxtaposed. Each term of the opposition is blunted by containing its own contrary, for Keats is shaping the terms, not to mark the dichotomy, but to nudge them towards a fusion. Hence, all the sense of transient action in the last three lines, since it has been communicated by a motionless marble relief, is properly carried by nouns and adjectives rather than by verbs. The apparently transitory movement does not take place; it is named or described as though it were captured and held rigid. We do not hear the tune, but see the instruments; the men do not pursue, but there is pursuit; the maidens are not struggling, but there is struggle; and the tension between "struggle" and "escape" further moves the activity towards a taut stasis. A slight acceleration of slow time would put the apparently static urn in the flowing current of change; and a slight tug would wholly remove from time the apparently energetic figures of the frieze. Like the humanity and/or divinity of the figures, like the marriage-chastity of the urn and the virginity-ravishment of the maidens, the immortality of the urn and the temporality of the figures are delicately poised on each side of heaven's bourne, yearning towards that area of mystic interfusion to which solitary thinkings can mount "—but no more."

The only linkage between the frieze and the urn is made by the line "What leaf-fring'd legend haunts about thy shape" (5), and the paradoxical vagueness of the words "haunts about" makes that relationship fluid, malleable, instead of fixed. The frieze is not superimposed upon the urn or juxtaposed to it; it is the spectral essence that is independent of the urn and yet, at the same time, is diffused through the urn's atmosphere. This paradox of indwelling and independence is the precondition for oxymoronic fusion. The long period making up the stanza, beginning softly and slowly, and becoming breathlessly excited in the staccato series of questions, finally reaches its climax in the words "wild ecstasy." The ecstasy brings together the pursuit and the music, the human and the superhuman, and, by conveying an impression of exquisite sense-spirit intensity, leads us to that fine edge between mortal and immortal where passion is so intense that it refines itself into the essence of ecstasy, which is without passion. "Ecstasy" is therefore both the end towards which the dramatic action of the symbols has been moving, and also the means of entry into the second stanza.

In the second stanza all the nearly antithetical elements of the first now rush together and coalesce. There is song; and yet it is unheard, is played to the spirit, and has no tone—that is, none of those accidents that impart to the essence of song a distinctive and audible quality, and yet whose removal does not deny the song-ness. . . . The silence of the urn and the sound of the pipes and timbrels have run together. The chastity and marriage of the urn, the pursuit and escape of the human figures, are also resolved in an area where time blends with no-time; where the infinity of "For ever wilt thou love, and she be fair!" (20) is born out of the immediacy of "never canst thou kiss, / Though winning near the goal" (17-18).

The marriage-chastity of the urn and the virginity-ravishment of the maidens now intermingle: the lover can never kiss, though winning near the goal, and yet he will love for ever. Urn and maidens have coalesced in this chaste ravishing, for, by being stretched out into an infinity of time, the passionate pursuit can never be completed to become a destruction. The maidens now partake of the "still unravish'd" condition of the urn, not because, like the urn, they are untouched by the ravishing, but because the pursuit is protracted into infinity. On one side there is loving; on the other, loved. But between lies the vital essence of love, a ravishing that can never become ravishment.

II

Before we can follow further the dramatic action of the symbols, we must return to stanza one to gather up a cluster of images. The urn, we are told, is a "sylvan" historian, its tale "flowery," and its legend "leaf-fring'd." It is both outwardly and inwardly woodland, for the frieze has a border of leaves about it, and the scene depicted within the frieze is sylvan. Second, the men and maidens are in the throes of the love-pursuit. And finally the pipes and timbrels are the symbols of music. In the first stanza these images—trees, lovers, and song—hover just below the level of the main sense and appear in almost random positions. "Sylvan," "flowery," and "leaf-fring'd" are adjectival, perceptible only through the translucency of the nouns whose property they are. Only our fecund talent for recognizing the rapacity of love, and not anything in the explicit description, leads us to see the pursuit and struggle as a love-game instead of a brutality. . . . Finally, the pipes and timbrels are also somewhat slighted as they are shuffled into the rapid succession of love symbols. Through the tissue of the first stanza these three images are only emergent.

In the second stanza the originally subliminal images have become the central theme. The entire stanza works towards fixing the three images in heaven's bourne, where sound is so intense as to be inaudible, the maturation of nature so intense as to be without growth or decay, and the consummating of love so intense as to be without consummation. The images are now on the surface of the poetic texture, the least attention being given to the trees, more to the song, and most to the lovers; but they still tend to be scattered and intermingled, falling into no obvious pattern of relative significances.

To say, however, that the three images have emerged dramatically into a significance is to concentrate on the movement of the images alone. In the more obvious sense, the three images do evolve; in another, Keats and the reader are being drawn empathically into the action in the frieze, although the surface of the poem is wholly a drama of the symbols, and the poet's involvement in the drama appears only in the implications of the imagistic grammar. When the total personified urn is the object of attention at the beginning of stanza one, the three images are presented to a subordinate level of consciousness, just as they are subordinate physically to the real urn itself. But they loom larger in proportion as Keats, appearing only in the mode in which the action is expressed, increasingly enters into a participation in the life of the images. Or, conversely, Keats's emphatic participation in the images increases as the images grow larger upon the consciousness.

The key to a reading of the ode, then, is the perception of these triune movements in the first two stanzas: (1) the gradual emergence of the three images, (2) the gradual absorption of the poet into the three images, and (3) the convergence of the immortal-essential and the temporal-physical towards a point of fusion where these categorical distinctions are blotted out. These are not three parallel dramas, but different manifestations of the same one. The converging movements of the transitory and the eternal to the point where songs are refined of tone to become the vital essence of song, and the emphatic entrance of the poet into the essence of the scène, for example, exist only in each other.

III

In order to follow the action of the images into the third stanza, which largely because of the repetition of the word "happy," has usually been condemned as a sentimental lingering over the scene, it would be helpful to know the significance of this word in Keats's vocabulary. The clue . . . [is] in a passage in *Endymion* beginning, "Wherein lies happiness?" —a passage that he singled out as of extraordinary importance in the ways of his poetic mind. When I wrote it, he declared, "it was a regular stepping of the Imagination towards a Truth. My having written that Argument will perhaps be of the greatest Service to me of any thing I ever did. It set before me at once the gradations of Happiness even like a kind of Pleasure Thermometer." [4] The argument of the passage to which Keats refers is that "happiness" lies

> In that which becks
> Our ready minds to fellowship divine,
> A fellowship with essence; till we shine,
> Full alchemiz'd, and free of space. Behold
> The clear religion of heaven!

Happiness, then, is no cheap gaiety, but the *summum bonum,* the opposite of the weariness, the fever, and the fret that are the inherent attributes of the unhappy mortal world. It lies, we notice, *in* that which beckons us until we are free of the spatial, that extension which is the opposite of essence; and freedom from space begins at heaven's bourne, the point of mystic blending. If boughs can beckon us there, then happiness lies *in* them, just as we assume a greenness in leaves if they have within themselves the property of provoking in us a perception of greenness; and Keats, in his own vocabulary, has as much justification in calling the boughs "happy boughs" as we have in calling the leaves "green leaves." Indeed, to describe the boughs, instead of the self, as "happy" is linguistically consistent with Keats's premise of empathy, for the happiness resides not in the self, but in the object into which the self is transported and in which it experiences. We also notice that these things of happiness entice "Our ready minds to fellowship divine, / A fellowship with essence"—which is a more poetical way of expressing what I have described as Keats's emphatic entrance into the life of the frieze, the vital

[4] Letter to Taylor, January 30, 1818.

core of the urn. For lack of another term I am using the word "empathy" here to describe, not the ego's attribution of the modes of its own activity to outward forms, but the act of freeing the self of its identity and its existence in time and space, and consequently the act of mystic absorption into the essence of outward forms. In this latter sense the doctrine of empathy is one of the cardinal principles of Keats's poetic and religious creed. "Men of Genius," he declared, "are great as certain ethereal Chemicals operating on the Mass of neutral intellect—[but] they have not any individuality, any determined Character." . . .[5]

True perception of essence, it is clear, requires something more than a subjective perceptual relationship; it must result from a fellowship with essence, and this fellowship comes about through an alchemy whereby the poet's identity is destroyed. In the ode, therefore, as Keats moved to a more intimate and self-obliterating relationship with the urn and the figures on it, so, proportionately, their apparent oppositions—chastity-marriage, deities-mortals, pursuit-escape, song-no tone—were blotting each other out; and the unselfed Keats was entering into a fellowship with their vital inwardness in which these oppositions are resolved. As his empathy with outward forms increases, so the elements of their outward conflicts converge and fuse to become their essence.

But what are the gradations of happiness that are "a regular stepping of the Imagination towards a Truth"? First,

> Fold
> A rose leaf round thy finger's taperness,
> And soothe thy lips.

After this sensuous delight in nature,

> hist, when the airy stress
> Of music's kiss impregnates the free winds,
> And with a sympathetic touch unbinds
> Eolian magic from their lucid wombs.

If we "feel" these things—the beauty of nature and of music—or rather, if we can experience the essence of sensuous delights and then perceive the essence of greater values through the penetrating power of the imagination,

[5] Cf. Letter to Woodhouse, October 27, 1818.

that moment have we stept
Into a sort of oneness, and our state
Is like a floating spirit's. But there are
Richer entanglements, enthralments far
More self-destroying, leading, by degrees,
To the chief intensity: the crown of these
Is made of love and friendship, and sits high
Upon the forehead of humanity.
All its more ponderous and bulky worth
Is friendship, whence there ever issues forth
A steady splendour; but at the tip-top,
There hangs by unseen film, an orbed drop
Of light, and that is love: its influence,
Thrown in our eyes, genders a novel sense,
At which we start and fret; till in the end,
Melting into its radiance, we blend,
Mingle, and so become a part of it,—
Nor with aught else can our souls interknit
So wingedly: when we combine therewith,
Life's self is nourish'd by its proper pith,
And we are nurtured like a pelican brood.[6]

IV

The ode, I think, will now admit us into the presence of its mystery. The steps of "the Imagination towards a Truth" are the empathic entrances into rose leaf (the sensuous beauty of nature), into music (essence imaginatively gained through the medium of art), and into love (spiritual essence). And in the ode a similar pleasure thermometer has dramatically been emerging into vividness, ordering itself into the symbols of those three areas of the mutable world in which there is happiness because, although they are of this world, fellowship with their essence raises us beyond the misery of mutability by identifying us with "a sort of oneness," the mysterious core of life. Essence, however, is atemporal, whereas the pleasure thermometer, because it belongs to this side of heaven's bourne, is a chronological program of becoming. Since the ode is a poem of the atemporal, Keats must overcome the element of time implicit in the pleasure thermometer, and hence he transfers the sense of time to the reader's growing awareness, instead of introducing the symbols in a hier-

[6] *Ibid.*, 795-815.

archical sequence. The temporality now lies in the reader's becoming increasingly more conscious of the gradual unveiling of the symbols, all three of which may therefore emerge cotemporaneously. The frieze which contains the three symbols is thus as free from time as the heaven's bourne it symbolizes.

The corresponding symbols in the ode—trees, song, and lovers—lurk beneath the texture of the first stanza and are scattered; come to the surface in the second and are apportioned their relative significances, but remain in disorder. And in the third stanza they become discrete and dramatically fall into proper place. Each of the first two symbols, trees and song, is there housed in its own distinct two-line unit (in contrast to the uninterrupted flow of the first stanza), and each of the two-line units is sharply end-stopped to mark off the emphatic progression of the symbols:

> Ah, happy, happy boughs! that cannot shed
>   Your leaves, nor ever bid the Spring adieu;
> And, happy melodist, unwearied,
>   For ever piping songs for ever new.

The third symbol—the "orbed drop / Of light" which is love—is also housed in its own end-stopped unit, but the unit is appropriately extended to three lines (and is followed by an appendage to be considered shortly). The passage in *Endymion* makes it clear that the three symbols are not equally spaced on the pleasure thermometer, but that the first two are the means of entry into that vast range at the top of which is love; and the distribution of the lines in stanza three of the ode (2, 2, 3 +) corresponds to that difference. Since happiness lies *in* each symbol because we are full alchemized only by a self-destroying entrance *into* the symbol until we "Mingle, and so become a part of it," then each symbol is properly described as happy. But the highest of these intensities is therefore surrounded by a clustering repetition of the word and is, moreover, "*More* happy love! *more* happy, happy love!" In its Keatsian sense the repetition of "happy" conveys an emphatic experience that is nervously taut.

In the first three stanzas there is also a drama of rhythms that coincides in its movement with that outward drama wherein the three symbols emerge from obscurity, grope about in the second stanza for a spiritual cosmos, and triumphantly secure a clear-cut, lucid order in the third. By this coincidence the rhythmical pattern also helps convey the significance of the more overt development of the images. First, the swelling tempo of the first stanza, accelerated by the staccato breaking of the questions, gives way to the slower harmony of the second, and then smoothes itself out in the orderly, sharply comparted phrasing of the third. The final sense of a controlled order in the third stanza is aided by the slow, deliberate movement that results from the clear ordonnance, from the repetition of "happy," and from the recurrence of the two patterns: "Ah, happy boughs . . . happy melodist . . . happy love," and "For ever piping . . . for ever new . . . For ever warm . . . For ever panting . . . for ever young." Second, the suggestion of disorder in the rhymes of the first sestet (cdedce) persists in those of the second (cdeced); but the sestet of the third stanza (cdecde) conveys the same sense of the unfolding of a spiritual harmony that is to be found in this stanza in the ordering of the symbols, the neat grouping of the rhetorical units, and the retarding of the tempo.

However, to read the first three stanzas only as a drama among the symbols, we have noted, is to see the drama in only one of its manifestations, for an implied drama between the poet and the symbols is also being unfolded, a drama that is conveyed by the mode of expression rather than by its substance. The evolution of the symbols is also the subtle involution of the poet. There are two of these empathic dramas being enacted in the first three stanzas. One, the self-destruction of the images in order that they may symbolize the dynamic stasis and the selflessness of heaven's bourne, quickly comes to a climax in the first stanza; the other, the unselfing of the poet by his entry into the unselfed symbols, occupies all three of the stanzas. The first of the two empathic movements centers about the word "ecstasy." We have already seen that, in the sense of "the most exquisite passion," the word tends, after the strenuous action of "pursuit" and "struggle," to draw together the mortal and immortal symbols toward a point of fusion so that in the next stanza the poet may move into an empathy with them and fix them in timeless activity. But in the sense of "the passage of the soul out of the self" (*ἐκ* + *ἱστάναι* = to make stand outside) it describes the consummation of the symbols' empathic act. That the word had this significance to Keats is clear from lines in the *Ode to a Nightingale:*

> While thou art pouring forth thy soul abroad
> In such an ecstasy!

The poet's own empathic advance is externalized, in part, by the contraction of his attention as it moves from the total urn in the opening lines, to the frieze on the urn, to the intense activity in the frieze. The sequence becomes organic instead of artificial by the personification of the urn: "Thou still unravish'd bride." Because of the personification Keats can establish a quasi-human rapport with the urn, who can then introduce him to the persons on its frieze. "What men or gods are these?" he asks the personified urn, as he moves one degree into its inner existence. The apostrophe makes the urn a circle within the poet's circle; the question makes the two circles coincide. In the second stanza, no longer regarding the total urn, he addresses the symbols directly as he is enfolded still further into the core of the urn: "ye soft pipes, play on," "Fair youth . . . thou canst not leave / Thy song." He is now inside the frame of the urn, coincident with the figures of its frieze. Finally, in the third stanza he has fully entered into the dynamically static existence of the symbols themselves as he does not merely address them, but, by means of the ecstatic exclamations, participates in their sensations and experiences. The poet has become engaged not only in the urn, but also in the frieze, and even in the life of the figures themselves as the psychic distances are destroyed and art becomes reality. Indeed, the reality has become vicarious experience.

This empathic movement of the poet's consciousness from consideration of the urn as total object to a participation in the inwardness of the symbols also has a modal enactment so that it is conveyed not only by observable gestures but also by the verbal form in which those gestures are couched. Let us suppose a scale of grammatical moods arranged in order of the increasingly empathic relationships they establish between subject and predicate. The least empathic, the most remote, is the interrogative, since it only asks that some sort of nexus be formed between subject and predicate. The implication that something is not known makes that something distantly remote from the subject and places between subject and predicate the person questioned. This is the degree of the poet's separation from the symbols at the conclusion of stanza one, especially as his questions have the air of being rhetorical and promise never to be answered. The two next more empathic moods are mingled in the second stanza. Here the indicative ("Heard melodies are sweet," "thou canst not leave / Thy son," etc.) implies that the subject has knowledge of the predicate; and the imperative ("play on," "Pipe," "do not grieve") assumes that the relationship is now so intimate that the subject may impel the predicate to an action. These imperatives are further reinforced by the vocatives ("ye soft pipes," "Fair youth," "Bold Lover"), for the vocative is to the noun as the imperative is to the verb. At the height of these empathic moods is the exclamatory, for it assumes that the subject is engaging in the life of the predicate—has mingled, "and so become a part of it." Keats now experiences the happiness of the symbols and knows, not objectively, but in his newly-acquired subjectivity, that the boughs cannot shed their leaves and that the love is "For ever warm and still to be enjoy'd." With the increasing intensities of the pleasure thermometer there has been integrated proportionately a scale of modal intensities so that the subjective and the objective intensities are correlated and made interdependent.

There is also a third aspect of the drama of the poet's absorption, in addition to the movement of his consciousness and the modal forms in which the movement is expressed. This third is a drama of grammatical subordination and independence. In the first stanza, we have seen, the three symbols are in a subordinate grammatical form or are subordinate to their full eventual semantic values; in the second the symbols are in a clearly defined independent form and are related to oxymoronic conditions which are expressed in equally independent form: "Heard melodies are sweet, but those unheard / Are sweeter; therefore, ye soft pipes, play on." But in the climactic third stanza Keats must enter into heaven's bourne, not merely describe it objectively. He must assimilate its nature in proportion as he enters more deeply into this region and consequently as its nature becomes more intimately a part of him. Therefore in the third stanza the statements of the nature of heaven's bourne slip from independent to subordinate form and thereby fall somewhat below the main level of conscious attention, just as the images themselves had been subliminal in the first stanza. "That cannot shed / Your leaves" is adjectival and is perceptible only through the independence of the image "boughs," and the same relationship applies to "For ever piping songs for ever new" and "melodist," "For ever warm and still to be enjoy'd" and "love." The conditions of heaven's bourne have been assimilated into the life of the symbols and of the poet, for at the height of the pleasure thermometer, as a consequence of the inter-knitting of the soul with essence,

> Life's self is nourish'd by its proper pith,
> And we are nurtured like a pelican brood.

Just as the legendary pelican partakes of the blood (essence) of its mother, who is physically distinct from her offspring although essentially the same, so through increasing intensities and enthrallments human life may ultimately be nourished in spirit by partaking of the nature of heaven's bourne, from which it is necessarily separated by that "fragile bar / That keeps us from our homes ethereal" [7] but to which human life belongs in its essential nature. What Keats has in mind is something approximately Eucharistic, and it is this Eucharistic act that is reflected in the adjectival absorption of the oxymoronic nature of heaven's bourne in stanza three.

The early part of this chapter sufficiently describes the third manifestation of the dramatic course in the first three stanzas—that is, the convergence of the mortal and immortal, or the Dionysian and Apollonian, to a point of interpenetration, along with the attendant deceleration of rhythms from the eager excitement of the first stanza to the slower harmony of the second and to the careful and neat deliberation of the third. But it must now be added that this is an insufficient account, for heaven's bourne is not a region of inertia, but of a stasis that at the same time is dynamic. Its immutability arises from an intensity of stress, not from the absence of it. And correspondingly, the leisurely pace and orderly grouping of the rhetorical units in stanza three are contained in exclamations, that is, in the most passionate and disorderly of the moods. The increasing Apollonian ordonnance that marks the emergence of the symbols out of their original obscurity and disorder, and the countercurrent of this increasing ordonnance—the increasing Dionysian intensity that marks the progress of the poet from mild wonderment to selfless ecstasy—have now come together at their climax. But here there is no clash between the dynamic and the static. There was such an opposition in the first stanza, for there the two qualities were conveyed by juxtaposed symbols seeking a reconciliation with each other. But as form and content always tend to absorb each other into an organic union, flux and stasis—the ecstatic content and the neat ordering—blend into a powerful tension in stanza three to reflect the Dionysian-Apollonian character of heaven's bourne.

Yet even this account does not fully describe Keats's amazingly complex treatment of the dynamic and the static, for he not only regulates the tempo of his rhythms to control the meaning of his poem, but also deals directly with the subject of time. It is especially pertinent that he do so, since the ideal condition towards which the first movement of the poem

[7] *Ibid.*, 360-61.

strives is one in which all the intense activities of the temporal world continue to exist, but outside the context of time. What Keats seeks is the steadfastness of the bright star, but not its "lone splendour"; instead, he aspires to be

> still steadfast, still unchangeable,
> Pillow'd upon my fair love's ripening breast,
> To feel for ever its soft fall and swell,
> Awake for ever in a sweet unrest.[8]

Towards this timeless and changeless intensity the deceleration of chronological time ("slow time") in the first stanza is moving. The second stanza then places the symbols at heaven's bourne and therefore in a context of an infinitude of time. Here this endless timefulness is conveyed in the manner in which it is intelligible to the mutable world of extensions: that is, by absolutely denying something's not continuing to exist. This is the construction of "thou canst not [ever] leave / Thy song," "nor ever can those trees be bare," and "She cannot [ever] fade." The three verbs (leave, be bare, fade), each one corresponding to one of the three central symbols, have to do with passage from earthly existence; and the negation of these verbs therefore creates an infinity of mutable or chronological time, an absolute extension of the time that passes. From the point of view of the world, infinitude is merely the denial of the finitude of earthly being. It appears that the poet is in the dimensional world contemplating heaven's bourne, and hence must translate its atemporality into dimensional concepts. However, in the last line of this stanza and in stanza three the poet has himself entered into the realm where time exists in its essence and therefore is without extension. This is the sense conveyed by the repetition of the boldly positive assertion "For ever": "For ever wilt thou love," "For ever piping songs for ever new," "For ever warm," "For ever panting, and for ever young." It is as though the double negatives of stanza two, denying the cessation of worldly existence, constitute the only conceivable human definition of an infinite extension which in its repetition at heaven's bourne is known positively because it is without extension. The difference is that between infinite timefulness and the infinitude of absolute time. Into this extensionless time are assimilated the piping of the songs and the warmth and panting of the love, which cannot be conceived without reference to chronological time; and the fusion forms the nature of heaven's bourne, where the fall and swell of

[8] "Bright star! would I were steadfast as thou art."

"love's ripening breast" is caught up in the immutability of the lone star. There, becoming and being are one.

The temporal theme we have been following is also subtly symbolized in the first three stanzas by means of the subject of love and the love-act. In stanza one, we have seen, the long-continued purity of the urn-bride was juxtaposed with the imminent ravishment of the virginal maidens to reveal that in the mutable world only the unvital can approach the timeless because, being itself without action, it is not touched by the destructiveness of the temporal act; and that the vital, even though it seeks to remain outside the framework of mutability, is, by being vital (and therefore mortal), in imminent danger of destruction by act, for in the temporal world action is always becoming its own past tense. Only the unvital can be immutable; the vital must pass. And the state the poem is moving towards is one of timeless vitality, an immortality of passion, an oxymoronic fusion of the urn and the maidens.

The conditions of the two images are then brought together in stanza two but are viewed from the perspective of the mutable world, just as the infinity of time was interpreted in terms of worldly extension: "She cannot fade, though thou hast not thy bliss" (19). The maiden is as vitally virginal as in stanza one, but now, time having been extended infinitely, she is also as unvitally unravished as the urn. But in the world of mutability the normal consequence of having bliss is a fading; and therefore an immortality of passion, a virginal ravishment, can be conceived of only by paradoxically abrogating this normal causal relationship: *even though* the lover cannot enjoy the act of love, the maiden is an immortality of passion and he will love forever.

Finally, in the climactic third stanza the oxymoronic condition is consummated, both the temporal and atemporal conceptions of an immortality of passion being fused in the ambiguity of the line "For ever warm and still to be enjoy'd" (26). From the temporal point of view of the mortal world, the love is still (yet) *to be* enjoyed; the maiden is passionately vital because she has not yet been ravished, and the lover will love forever because he cannot have his bliss. From an atemporal point of view, the love is *still* (forever) to be enjoyed. The presence of both meanings in the ambiguity of the line fuses the temporal and the atemporal, the mortal and the immortal. No longer must the lover forego the kiss, as in stanza two, in order that the maiden be eternally fair and that he love forever. The enjoying is an act that occupies a timeless eternity, and yet paradoxically it is unaffected by time because it is yet to become a temporal act.

It has already been observed that although the drama of the first three stanzas has been separated here into three strands for the purpose of analysis, within the poem the three are coextensive. The empathic involvement of the poet is only the dramatic emergence of the symbols seen from a bias; and the progress towards a condition of mystic oxymoron is itself the emergence of the symbols and the annihilation of the poet's identity. This triunity is finally captured at the climax of the entire movement in the density of the repeated word "happy" in stanza three. In one sense, the word is an account of heaven's bourne, for if the symbols are happy, then in them lies the power to beckon the ready mind "to fellowship divine, / A fellowship with essence," and therefore to free one from space—that mutable extension that characterizes this world although not heaven's bourne. Moreover, the symbols themselves are also happy in their having attained heaven's bourne, where ultimate happiness is to be found in an eternality of passionate experience. Yet, in the literal sense, of course, boughs cannot be happy except that by a pathetic fallacy, which is akin to empathy, Keats has transferred to them the "happiness" he experiences in participating in their perfect existence at heaven's bourne. Or, to accept Keats's own premises, the happiness is experienced by the poet by his entering into the life of the boughs, the happiness being an aspect of their existence. Thus, in this word all three manifestations of the drama are contained in their complete fulfillment.

V

In the third stanza, then, the first major movement of the poem has clearly reached a climax beyond which it cannot go, for the third stanza has exhausted all the potentialities of this movement and has left nothing more to be said. The poet, ecstatically unselfed into the symbols, is now partaking of the essence of life. If the poem is to continue, it must take a different direction and therefore result in a different intention. But if the statement that beauty is truth is the total intention of the poem, then surely it is here that it belongs, and no where else. For this is what the poem has been saying up to this point.

Beauty, it must be clear, is not an abstraction, but a beauty so exquisitely sensory as to be the sensuous essence of beauty—an inner and experiential intensity, not a form. Keats, I am convinced, could understand beauty only phenomenalistically—only as the sensory quality of the piping of songs and the warmth and panting of the lover. What "truth" means here I prefer not to say, except in the terms of the poem itself, with the aid of some confirmation by Keats's own statements elsewhere, although I think the dramatic movement of the poem alone impels one to intuit the meaning clearly enough. Truth certainly is not to be grasped by "consecutive reasoning," nor by an exertion of the will. One certainly cannot attain it by pursuing it as a goal: Dilke, Keats wrote, "will never come at a truth as long as he lives; because he is always trying at it." Contrarily, then, truth is as much the reward of "negative capability"—the power to have no self—as the penetration into essence is; and this penetration into essence is the act of perceiving beauty. Therefore Keats held that "What the imagination seizes as Beauty must be truth—whether it existed before or not." It was this experiential nature of truth that Keats had in mind when he wrote that "axioms in philosophy are not axioms until they are proved upon our pulses." . . . If the perception of beauty and the perception of truth are fundamentally the same act, and if the sensory experiences of the pleasure thermometer lead not only to heaven's bourne, but also to truth, then beauty and truth are different in degree, not in kind, or are different conditions of the same thing.

Let us simply say, then, that beauty is the condition of being that extends up to heaven's bourne and includes it, and that truth is the condition of being that begins with heaven's bourne and continues beyond it. In heaven's bourne they meet, for there the sensory experience of beauty is divested of time, space, and identity, and therefore of all that makes it untrue in this world. When, consequently, we have seen it enacted in the ode that the love is "For ever warm and still to be enjoy'd," we might well conclude that therefore beauty is truth. That the aphorism is delayed until after the poem has taken a different direction should make us suspect that it has a somewhat different and less significant role to play in proportion as the remaining dramatic action qualifies the enactment in the first three stanzas of the fact that at heaven's bourne beauty is truth.

VI

The new direction taken by the action is not distinct from the first, but arises organically out of it, as antithesis arises out of thesis. Having gained full empathic entrance into essence, and having been carried by that essence to the height of the scale of intensities, Keats is at last able to experience a nature which is forever becoming and so cannot bid the

Spring adieu, and song which is forever the same and yet forever new. His attaining the height—the orbed drop of light that is love—causes him to prolong his ecstasy beyond that aroused by nature and song: "For ever warm and still to be enjoy'd, / For ever panting, and for ever young." And Keats would continue in this fellowship with essence—if he could. So long as he can conceive of heaven's bourne as an organic fusion—temporal warmth, enjoyment, panting, and youth that are caught up in atemporality—he may safely remain there in his vision.

But his next account of this area is a powerful drama of meaningful ambiguities whose struggle with each other eventually filters out the mortal from the immortal, the mutable from the immutable, beauty from truth. Fundamentally, it is a drama of syntax, for it appears that instead of continuing to coalesce opposites by absorbing one into another, Keats has stumbled into expressing the oxymoronic condition by opposing contraries: "All breathing human passion far above." The tendency of the reader's mind is to smooth out the syntax: the passion of the lovers, it half feels, is far above human passion and distinct from it. And yet Keats's intention is to say precisely that the love is "All breathing human passion far above," for this is the syntactical analogue of the mystic oxymoron. The love is indeed a human passion, and at the same time it is far above all mutable human passion, for at heaven's bourne mortal and immortal, the temporal and atemporal, beauty and truth, are one. . . . But unlike the oxymoronic pattern of "For ever warm and still to be enjoy'd," which organically assimilates a temporal act into an atemporal texture through an ambivalence of meaning, the syntactical oxymoron is synthetic, for it is positional and therefore the meaningful inversion is ready to dissolve into a mere opposition of "human passion" and "far above." The fine coalescence of the antithetical conditions, one feels, is too strenuous for the merely conceptual mind to sustain, and it threatens to disintegrate upon the least incaution, even an incaution in choice of syntax.

At first glance, like the poet himself, we do not see that he has stumbled, for the line seems inevitable enough, and the words "human passion" appear in an inconspicuous position. But the line produces not only the meaningful ambiguity nicely calculated to express the fusion of the human and the superhuman, but also a certain degree of bewilderment, which the poet seems to share. Could it mean that the passion is human and yet is far above that human passion that leaves a heart high-sorrowful? or that something far above human passion leaves a heart high-sorrowful? or that there is something far above human passion, and it is human passion which leaves a heart high-sorrowful? At any rate, the damage has been done, and out of the bewildering disintegration of the syntax comes an unexpected attention to merely human passions and the sobering recollection that they leave a "heart high-sorrowful and cloy'd, / A burning forehead, and a parching tongue." It appears that the poet has not created the confusion, but that the unstable situation his vision created has bewildered him in the midst of his ecstasy and forced him into a direction that he did not intend or expect. The recollection of the mortal world is calling him back to his sole self and is filtering out of heaven's bourne its component parts. On the one side is the immutability of "far above"; on the other are the agony and the impermanence attendant upon the experience of intensity in this world.

Out of this fracturing of heaven's bourne the next movement of the drama springs. Continuing to participate in the activity of the frieze, Keats now asks three questions. The first, like those of the first stanza, asks for identity: "Who are these coming to the sacrifice?" But of course there can be no answer, for at heaven's bourne there is only selflessness. The next two questions then introduce a new and significant element into the poem; they ask for directions: *to* what green altar is the sacrificial procession going? and *from* what town has it come? These are spatial questions and can no more be answered than those of identity, for heaven's bourne is essential space. The result of fellowship with essence is that we become "Full alchemiz'd, and free of space." . . .

The altar and town are therefore dimensional points as irrelevant to heaven's bourne as they are absent from the frieze. The procession itself is frozen in space and time on the urn: it can never arrive at the altar; it can never return to the town. It is poised between heaven and earth, and is the "element filling the space between." However, in the poet's mind the scene has now thawed and its frozen dimensions have begun to flow, for although the poet's attention is being concentrated on the spaceless procession, he is now imagining its before and after. The heaven's bourne of stanza three has been translated into the mutable world; the figures of the frieze have been extracted from the world of art and are being examined in the light of mutable reality. The symbols of the third stanza had acted in absolute time and space, but, mortal and immortal having now been separated out of heaven's bourne by the recollection of human passions, the poet sees the same procession in earthly, and therefore dimensional, space and time. In stanza three the theme had been that between doing and done lies the eternally vital act—the essence of growth, song, and love. In stanza four the theme is that at each moment in the extensional world, act is either doing or done. And the figures of the first three stanzas, when now observed in a spatial and temporal context, must expend their dynamic movement by having places from which to come and to which to go, a beginning and an end.

The priest who leads the procession is doubly mysterious: he is as much without identity as the other figures at heaven's bourne; and in addition he is to conduct a religious mystery. The sacrificial altar towards which the procession goes is, then, dedicated to heaven, to a realm of pure spirit: the immortal without the mortal, truth without beauty. And the town that the souls leave is the town all souls leave in their human progress towards the heaven-altar. Only the dynamically static figures appear on the urn, only heaven's bourne is depicted there; but the now dimension-bound mind of the poet, no longer able to hold mortal and immortal in oxymoronic fusion, divides it imaginatively into its component symbols: the heaven-altar and the world-town. And he thrusts them to the opposite extremes of the scene. The component parts were also separate in stanza one as men and gods, chastity and marriage, quiet and ecstasy, but they were converging towards a union. In stanza four, however, the oppositions have been separated out only to move farther apart and become irreconcilable: the souls, having left the sensory realm in their journey to the heaven-altar, can never return to explain the world's desolation, its division from heaven's bourne, the impossibility of the soul's remaining eternally on earth. For in the mutable world in which the poet has now imaginatively enfolded the sacrificial procession, time and space create only one universal history: a passage of souls from the world-town to a heaven-altar, from which there is no return. At heaven's bourne all eternally is; in the mutable world, all passes. And therefore it cannot be from man's own total history that man will learn the purpose for which the soul must leave the world desolate. If he is to learn that purpose, it must be by other means.

Most of stanza four is devoted to the town, for the recollection of human passion is calling upon the poet to make a commentary upon the mortal world, not the realm of pure spirit. Yet Keats does not hate the world for not being a heaven. To him it is the source of rich beauty, an opportunity for an enthrallment in the essence of the sensuous; and it differs from heaven in its condition of being, not in its kind. It must, then, be viewed with loving tenderness for what it is—and yet with pity for all it is not. The town, he emphasizes, is little; the word "street" sounds small against the spaceless sweep of the first three stanzas; unlike the men-gods, those eternal youths who have been the actors in the drama up to this point, the inhabitants are only humble "folk"; and "emptied" not only has a hollow and barren ring, but, like the word "little," underscores the spatial extension of the mutable world, in which it is possible to speak of size or to remove something and leave a void. Instead of the vital tension of selfless ecstasy at heaven's bourne, the self-enclosing and therefore anti-empathic "citadel" is only "peaceful" in the solemnity of the "pious morn." The town is now desolate (ambiguously both "sad" and "alone") because the soul has completely escaped the mortal form to leave a worldly desolation.

Moreover, the word "silent" works like a thread to integrate the stanza ironically with the rest of the poem. In stanza one, silence results from an amplitude of extension; by enduring in time, the urn is tending to draw thin the extensions of the world in which it exists and so is related to quietness, silence, and slow time. Because extensions seem not to affect the urn, in a sense it is without these extensions. But this silence has been introduced mainly to lead us to another kind in stanza two; here silence is the absolute of sound, its vital essence, which can be made audible only by adding to it the accidents of the dimensional world. In stanza four, however, we are fully back in the mortal world, where silence results only from the removal of sound. In stanza two, not to hear is to hear most essentially; now, not to hear is to have nothing to hear. The soul having withdrawn from physical matter, there is an everlasting void in sound, just as there is also a void in space: the streets for evermore will silent be. In the last stanza the thread of this theme will appear once again as the "silent form" of the urn when at last we have returned to a silence like that of the opening stanza. (But, we shall see, this final silence will, in the very act of completing the circle of this theme, take on a new and much larger meaning.)

Finally, the theme of time is also woven into stanza four in the words "for evermore" (38) and "[not] e'er" (40) produce the same ironic inversion of meaning. In stanza two the atemporality of heaven's bourne was conceived in dimensional terms; negating the absence of dimension created an infinite dimension and thus a plenitude of chronological time. But in stanza three the atemporality was seen directly from heaven's bourne, and the sense of that essence of time was dinned into the reader's mind by the regular recurrence of the words "for ever." However, only not-being can truly be chronologically infinite in the mutable world, and it was for this reason that a complex periphrasis had been required in stanza two to express the chronological infinitude of essential being. At heaven's bourne Being itself—the essential "ditties of no tone"—exists in essential time; however, only the absence of sound can truly be eternal in the world. At heaven's bourne act never becomes done—"For ever wilt thou love" "though thou hast not thy bliss." But in the extensional world of stanza four, where only not-being can be infinite, everness can truly come only *after* the act is done: "and not a soul . . . can e'er return" and "thy streets for evermore / Will *silent* be."

Just as the progress toward heaven's bourne in the first three stanzas involved the gradual absorption of the poet's identity, so the fracturing and dispersion of the oxymoronic factors involve the retreat of the poet from the completely self-annihilating empathy of stanza three, until he is again contracted within his own citadel-like self. In one sense, the empathy is as great in stanza four as in stanza three, for the poet is still so greatly assimilated into the life and reality of the figures of the frieze that he can concern himself with their origin and destination; and the repetition in the sestet of stanza four of the orderly configuration of rhymes in stanza three (cdecde) suggests this relationship of the two stanzas. But the very act of placing the figures in a spatial context and of conceiving of them imaginatively in a framework more extensive than the frieze necessarily implies a degree of separation between the poet and the symbols. Consequently stanza four inverts the previous empathic direction and traces the return route from stanza three back to one. Although the return to the interrogative mood in stanza four suggests the empathic remoteness of stanza one, the poet is here questioning, not the urn, but no specific addressee; and hence, although the question "Who are these coming to the sacrifice?" divorces the poet from the figures, no barrier has yet been intruded between them. The poet has now withdrawn sufficiently so that he can next address the mysterious priest, one of the figures, and thereby he has retreated beyond the distance in stanza two, for the relationship of poet to figures is now merely that of subject to predicate, the priest standing between the two. Having sufficiently withdrawn from the figures inside the frieze to question one of them, he next arrives at a point midway between the frieze and the total urn, for the little town that he addresses, although an image provoked by the poet's participation in the activity within the frieze, exists only in his own imagination.

This movement then reaches its fulfillment in stanza five. There the poet has retreated fully from all engagement in the urn, is wholly self-contained, and is once again, as in stanza one, addressing the total personified urn: "Fair attitude" (i.e., beautiful pose). Proportionately as the poet withdraws, the figures in the frieze take on greater psychic distance. Once vitally engaged in a foreverness of passionate activity, they shrink from view as they are surrounded by the imagined symbols of town and altar, and finally in stanza five freeze to marble, become lifeless embroidery superimposed on the urn instead of dynamic values at the heart of the urn. And they therefore slip into the same subordinate grammatical position they occupied in stanza one: "*with* brede / Of marble men and maidens," "*With* forest branches and the trodden weed." The dissolution of the mystic oxymoron which is heaven's bourne, the descent of the symbols, and the retreat of the poet are, like their opposites, a single dramatic movement.

VII

We can now see the two major interlacing patterns of the ode. The first pattern makes the five stanzas perfectly symmetrical and brings the poem round full circle. The empathic progress, the evolution of the symbols, and the convergence upon heaven's bourne move forward in the first two stanzas; in the third and central stanza they all come to a climax and find the origin of their dissolution; and they fall away to their original condition in the remaining two, the full return of the circle being marked by the return in the last stanza to the rhyme-pattern of the first (cdedce). But this is only the formal orientation of the drama of the ode into the artistic neatness of perfect structural balance; and if we consider this complete circular movement alone, the drama seems to have taken us on a perilous journey only to return us to the point from which we started. We appear to have traveled to heaven's bourne only to return home and know that our journey was futile. Within this pattern, however, another is operative that gives the drama its meaning.

Like the first stanza, the fourth is made up largely of rhetorical questions; and the last stanza, like the third, is largely exclamatory; and into both stanzas four and five are absorbed declarative statements like those of three. It is as though, after the climax in stanza three, Keats were beginning the movement of the poem all over again; as though, having completed his independent clause in the first three stanzas, he were now qualifying it with a dependent clause which will have approximately the same rhetorical form as the independent clause but which will invert the direction of the symbols and the poet's empathy. This pattern suggests the two waves of the Italian sonnet, a form with which Keats had recently been experimenting, for the second wave, although weaker, is carried by the impetus of the first to a resolution the first could not attain. As the first movement dissolves beneath it, this second and briefer sweep of the poem, moving rhetorically in the same course as the first, will climb forward to find for the first movement its meaning.

VIII

What, then, are we to make of the statement that beauty is truth, the statement incorporated into the exclamations of stanza five, just as there is a statement nestled among the questions of stanza four? The first three stanzas have acted out a vitality that is eternal, a passionate foreverness, a beauty that is truth. But we have already seen these conditions disintegrate in stanza four into a complete separation of world and spirit as the poet withdrew his self into the mortal and dimensional world. Having slipped back into only mortal comprehension and thereby having extended his consciousness around essence to embrace the spatial and temporal aspects of an eternity of passion—aspects which he sees as the symbolic town and altar—the poet has concluded stanza four with an assertion that contradicts the first three stanzas: the "streets for evermore / Will silent be; and not a soul to tell / Why thou art desolate, can e'er return." From the perspective of this world, spirit deserts the passionate existence; passion is mortal, and immortality does not embrace our sensory world. To put it bluntly, stanza three has said that at heaven's bourne beauty is truth; and stanza four has said that in this world beauty is not truth, truth is not beauty. If there is to be a consistent meaning in the poem, it must appear in a synthesis that reconciles the thesis of the first three stanzas and the antithesis in stanza four.

Surely, then, it cannot be the total intent of the poem to reveal merely that beauty is truth at heaven's bourne, for in stanza four the poem has said more than this. Nor, assuming now that the intention comprehends all of the last two lines of the poem, can it be the purpose to say that the sum total of earthly wisdom is the knowledge that beauty is truth at heaven's bourne and that this knowledge is sufficient. What the poem has been acting out is that this is the maximum wisdom, not the minimal—a bare sufficiency. Moreover, to know that beauty is identical with truth is not worldly wisdom, for the identity is a condition that does not exist here; and the knowledge therefore can be of no immediate aid within the confines of this life. Nor can it be that the identification of beauty and truth is an *experience* that embraces all the knowledge available to man *on earth,* a higher wisdom, presumably, being accessible hereafter; this is considerably more, not less, than stanza three admits, and it has been denied symbolically in stanza four. What is meant must be several removes from this, and in the opposite direction. If man is to "know" that beauty is truth, he must learn it, not by direct experience, but indirectly; it must be told him by the urn ("to whom thou say'st"), for otherwise he could not know it, since it is not true of the sphere of his direct experience and since no soul ever returns to tell the purpose for which the soul must abandon the mortal sphere. But the urn can divulge that purpose.

The intention of the poem, therefore, must be to hold up art as the source of the highest form of wisdom. It is in this more embracing sense, in addition to those we have already examined, that the urn has become in the final stanza a silent form which, although silent, paradoxically speaks to man. The very bourne of heaven does not noisily cry out to man its existence; knowledge of its nature is forever available, but man can gain it only by a self-annihilating entrance into the bourne itself. He may learn of the region of mystic oxymoron by being drawn into it, not by a direct communication of the mystery to him. . . . It is because the physical arts are less assertive than poetry and engage us directly in a sense-spirit experience instead of communicating and interpreting the experienced act that, I judge, the urn can tell its tale "more sweetly than our rhyme" (that is, than this poem, the ode), just as the assertive "heard melodies" are less sweet than those unheard. One of the grandeurs of immortality, Keats wrote, is that "there will be no space and consequently the only commerce between spirits will be by their intelligence of each other—when they will completely understand each other—while we in this world merely comprehend each other in different degrees." . . . Finally, art succeeds in drawing us into its essence—and thus in communicating—by teasing us "out of thought / As doth eternity" (44-45), for thought deals only with what is humanly conceivable and therefore limits one to the mutable world. Pan, we recall, is

> the unimaginable lodge
> For solitary thinkings; such as dodge
> Conception to the very bourne of heaven,
> Then leave the naked brain.

To enter into heaven's bourne we must circumvent the gravitational force of the conceptual mind, which would reduce the unimaginable to the imaginable, the unknown to the known. Yet, the silent communication of the essence of art teases us only out of thought; it does not substitute a different order of materials for those to which the conceptual mind is adequate. For heaven's bourne is made of the materials of conception existing under conditions that are beyond conception. . . .

IX

To return now to the concluding lines of the ode. Although the urn is able to reveal to man a oneness of beauty and truth, it is not able to inform him that this is the sum total of his knowledge on earth and that it is sufficient for his earthly existence ("all ye need to know"); for obviously he knows other things on earth, such as the fact that in the world beauty is not truth, and this should be even more valuable within the world than the knowledge that the two are one at heaven's bourne. But more important, the symbolic action of the drama at no point justifies the urn's limiting its message; nowhere has the urn acted out the fact that man knows no more on earth than this identity of beauty and truth, and that this knowledge is sufficient.

Now, it is significant that this is an ode *on* a Grecian urn. Had Keats meant *to,* he would have said so, as he did in the *Ode to a Nightingale.* There the meaning of the poem arises out of the dramatic relations of the poet and the symbol; but *on* implies a commentary, and it is Keats who must make the commentary on the drama that he has been observing and experiencing within the urn. It is the poet, therefore, who speaks the words, "that is all / Ye know on earth, and all ye need to know," and he is addressing himself to man, the reader. Hence the shift of reference from "thou" (urn) to "ye" (man). I do not feel the objection frequently raised that if the last line and a half belong to the poet and are addressed to the reader, they are not dramatically prepared for. The poet has gradually been obtruding himself upon the reader's consciousness in the last two stanzas by withdrawing from his empathic experience and taking on identity. He has become distintly present in the last stanza as a speaker addressing the urn, and proportionately the urn has shrunk from the center of dramatic interest; it is now but a short step for him to turn his address from urn to reader. Moreover, the reader has also been subtly introduced into the stanza, for the poet vividly marks his complete severance from the urn's essence by pluralizing himself ("tease us," "other woe / Than ours") and thus putting himself into a category wholly distinct from the urn; and by this act Keats has now involved the reader as a third member of the drama. Finally, when the reader has been filtered out of the plural "us" and "ours" by the reference to "man" (48), the poet may now address to him his final observations on the drama.

But the poet is no more justified than the urn would be in concluding that the sum of necessary earthly wisdom is the identity of beauty and truth. Certainly when he returned to the dimensional world in stanza four he found the two to be antithetical, not identical. . . . Then, since we have seen that the antecedent of "that" cannot reasonably be the aphorism—since neither urn nor poet can be saying that all man knows and needs to know on earth is that beauty is truth—its antecedent must be the entire preceding sentence.

All that man knows on earth, and all he needs to know is that

> When old age shall this generation waste,
> Thou [the urn] shalt remain, in midst of other woe
> Than ours, a friend to man, to whom thou say'st,
> Beauty is truth, truth beauty.

Only this meaning can be consistent with the dramatic action of the poem, for it not only does not deny that in the world beauty is not truth, but also assimilates that fact into a greater verity. The sum of earthly wisdom is that in this world of pain and decay, where love cannot be forever warm and where even the highest pleasures necessarily leave a burning forehead and a parching tongue, art remains, immutable in its essence because that essence is captured in a "Cold Pastoral," a form which has not been created for the destiny of progressing to a heaven-altar, as warm and passionate man is. This art is forever available as "a friend to man," a power willing to admit man to its "sphery sessions." The urn fulfills its friendship as the comedies and tragedies of Beaumont and Fletcher do, for, being the earthly souls of the dramatists, they, too,

> Teach us, here, the way to find you,
> Where your other souls are joying,
> Never slumber'd, never cloying.

They give us, that is, a prefigurative vision of a realm

> Where the nightingale doth sing
> Not a senseless, tranced thing.
> But divine melodious truth;
> Philosophic numbers smooth;

Tales and golden histories
Of heaven and its mysteries.[9]

The great end of poetry, Keats wrote, is "that it should be a friend / To sooth the cares, and lift the thoughts of man," [10] for art (unlike man, who cannot return to tell us of his postmortal existence) allows a glimpse into that region which shows the full meaning of those experiences which now produce only mortal suffering, divulges the end for which they are destined, and so eases the burden of the mystery. And art eases this burden by holding out to man the promise that somewhere—at heaven's bourne, where the woes of this world will be resolved—songs are forever new, love is forever young, human passion is "human passion far above," beauty is truth; that, although beauty is not truth in this world, what the imagination seizes as beauty must be truth—whether it existed before or not.

The knowledge that in art this insight is forever available is the height of earthly wisdom; and it is all man needs to know, for it endows his earthly existence with a meaning and a purpose. It provides him with "A hope beyond the shadow of a dream."

. . . thou must wander far
In other regions, past the scanty bar
To mortal steps, before thou cans't be ta'en
From every wasting sigh, from every pain,
Into the gentle bosom of thy love.
Why it is thus, one knows in heaven above.[11]

Or, like Keats, one may learn why by attending a sphery session of a Grecian urn.

[9] *Bards of Passion and of Mirth.*
[10] *Sleep and Poetry,* 245-57.
[11] *Endymion,* I. 857; II. 123-28.

Lamia

by David Perkins

In *Lamia* an analogous story [to that in *La Belle Dame Sans Merci*] also resulted in ambiguity. Lycius, of course, resembles the knight as he is briefly drawn into an affair with a "lady elf" or demon, and if Keats describes his plight with sympathy, he can also make use of Apollonius to voice a withering contempt. As in *La Belle Dame Sans Merci,* the attitude to Lamia seems to shift through the course of the poem, revealing an irresolution in Keats himself. But as compared with the odes, at least, both *La Belle Dame* and *Lamia* embody a more settled state of mind. The doubt concerns only what attitude to take in exposing the visionary imagination. The escape it offers may be sweet but impossible to possess for very long. Or, as in *Lamia,* the condemnation may be sterner in character, emphasizing that the vision deceives. The lover of vision may be only the innocent victim of his own quest for happiness, or he may be a fool as well. In any case, he is certain to become a "wretched wight." We may remember what Endymion comes to acknowledge:

> There never liv'd a mortal man, who bent
> His appetite beyond his natural sphere,
> But starv'd and died. (IV, 646-648)

The very opening of *Lamia* is in marked contrast with the *Ode on a Grecian Urn* and the *Ode to a Nightingale.* In these two odes, as in so much of Keats's earlier poetry, the desire or interest had been to bring together human life and the Greek pastoral or visionary world. Now, however, in the opening of *Lamia,* the over-all effect is to distinguish sharply between them. For the poem begins with a pretty love affair between the god Hermes and a nymph. There are elements, in this little prefatory idyl, that suggests the sort of ideal union represented or symbolized by the recurrent pairs of lovers in Keats's earlier poems. The difference is that now the whole affair is relegated to a nonhuman realm. With it, to some extent, is also relegated the issue that was a central concern in so much of Keats's earlier poetry: the hope of waking from a dream to find it actual. There is almost the suggestion that this awaking to find it truth, this authenticating of the visionary imagination, takes place only in the realm of myth, where dream and actuality are interchangeable. So Hermes, desiring to find the nymph, at last sees her—

> It was no dream; or say a dream it was,
> Real are the dreams of Gods, and smoothly pass
> Their pleasures in a long immortal dream. (I, 126-128)

Indeed, the significance of this episode, as Mr. Wasserman has said, is that the human world does not in any way participate in it.[1] By implication, the affair between Hermes and the nymph suggests the impossibility of any such fulfillment in the human world of process and mortality. This prefatory episode can have little purpose otherwise. It has no necessary, organic connection with the story that follows. In a rather artificial way, it is used to introduce the main story. But it is then dismissed.

We can only assume that this half-playful, slightly mocking idyl is to highlight, by contrast, the principal narrative. And the narrative that follows, whatever else can be said of it, is an exploration of the nature of illusion, and of the effect of disillusion on the human imagination. Significantly, none of the principal characters is a thoroughly desirable type. Lamia, the immortal serpent-woman, is no stable embodiment of the ideal: she is a shifting, evanescent thing, liable to vanish before the cold light of reason. Lycius, her mortal lover, is far from Shakespearean, to say the least; he has little to characterize him except an extraordinary capacity for wish-fulfillment, a desire to retreat with his vision, and a lack of flexibility. And the third principal character, Lycius's old tutor, Apollonius, whose sharp-eyed gaze penetrates to Lamia's true identity, makes her vanish by doing so, and thus indirectly kills his equally humorless pupil, has, aside from a certain dignity, only negative virtues to recommend him. He is free from illusions—at least of the visionary sort. But there is nothing positive; and he is almost as far as Lycius from approaching the ideal of the "mighty and miserable Poet of the human Heart," of which Keats spoke shortly before beginning *Lamia*. There is,

[1] *The Finer Tone*, pp. 159-162.

however, this difference. Whatever Apollonius represents cannot be disregarded. It must in some way be faced and subsumed.

Lamia is not quite of the same order as the god Hermes. But she is able to take on some of the same properties; and similarities are suggested. The god is described in terms of astronomical or heavenly images —"star of Lethe" or "bright planet"—and possesses a "serpent rod." Lamia is equally associated with astronomical images—for example, her "silver moons," "mooned body's grace," "stars," and "starry crown." The fact that Hermes and Lamia can each grant the love aspirations of the other suggests another similarity. But Lamia desires a mortal. She thus becomes a revised model of a familiar symbol—the immortal lady whose sexual union with a mortal symbolizes the human yearning to retain forever the apex of passionate intensity. She is La Belle Dame Sans Merci, the "faery's child," and so is described as a "lady elf," as having "elfin blood," and as lingering "faerily" by the roadside. The moon imagery links her with Cynthia. But she is also a serpent, which is to say that Cynthia has now become a serpent. In view of the many Miltonic echoes scattered through the poem, we may feel that, as a serpent, Lamia even suggests Satan.[2] At least, the Lamia theme may have attracted Keats because the serpent would be associated, however unconsciously, with temptation. Also Lamia is a "cruel lady" (though kind to the woodland nymph) with a "Circean head," and the reference to Circe suggests that she lures and seduces men to their own destruction.

But at least in the first part of the poem, she is described in a tone tinged with mockery. Hermes, for example, addresses her as a "beauteous wreath" and the periphrasis certainly shades into satire. The poet describes her as a grotesquerie:

> Striped like a Zebra, freckled like a pard,
> Eyed like a peacock, and all crimson barr'd. (I, 49-50)

The quick, college-cheer movement of the verse, the incongruity of the menagerie, and the kaleidoscope of color all define an attitude toward her. Moreover, her array of patterns and colors, "golden, green, and blue," shifts, flickers, and dazzles as she breathes, and together with her overlavish collection of other ornaments, her "silver moons" and her "crest

[2] Cf. the phrase "serpent prison-house" (line 203) with Keat's marginalia in *Paradise Lost* (IX, 179-191): "Satan having enter'd the Serpent, and inform'd his brutal sense—might seem sufficient—but Milton goes on . . . whose head is not dizzy at the possible speculations of Satan in the serpent prison?"

. . . Sprinkled with stars," it does not seem to be a highly tasteful display. She reminds one of a burlesque dancer. These wonders are topped by the bizarre absurdity of the mingling of woman and serpent.

> Her head was a serpent, but ah, bitter-sweet!
> She had a woman's mouth with all its pearls complete. (I, 59-60)

This is not far from caricature if one tries to visualize it; and the mocking humor is delicately enforced by calling attention to the "complete" set of "pearls" or teeth in her mouth. On the whole, this tone is maintained throughout the first half of the poem. Significantly, Keats, in opposition to his earlier antipathy to the style of Dryden and Pope, is now taking Dryden as a model. The gusto of Dryden, and his gift to ridicule, are caught up here, and they accentuate the ironic detachment. At the outset, then, the poet pictures Lamia as altogether mixed with contrarieties, and her ultimate attractions as highly ambiguous.

In her "serpent prison-house" Lamia was able to dream "of all she list," and "once, while among mortals dreaming thus, / She saw the young Corinthian Lycius." She "fell into a swooning love of him," and wants to make her dream a reality. Having adopted a woman's form, she is now "a maid / More beautiful" than any human maiden. She is paradoxically

> A virgin purest lipp'd, yet in the lore
> Of love deep learned to the red heart's core:
> Not one hour old, yet of sciential brain
> To unperplex bliss from its neighbour pain. (I, 189-192)

She seems to offer, that is, an escape from process to a pure bliss, unmingled with sorrow. Having stationed herself by the roadside, she calls to Lycius as he walks by, and he turns to her, at once seized with wonder and passion:

> For so delicious were the words she sung,
> It seem'd he had lov'd them a whole summer long:
> And soon his eyes had drunk her beauty up,
> Leaving no drop in the bewildering cup. (I, 249-252)

Here are the familiar symbols, song, summer, and wine, so frequently associated, as in the *Ode to a Nightingale,* with the movement into the world of vision. In this case, of course, the "bewildering cup" of Lamia's beauty merely suggests the wine symbolism. Lycius recognizes her as a "goddess" or immortal. The situation now begins to repeat the established pattern. Lycius fears that instead of his becoming united with the vision it will fade from his human eyes, and begs Lamia to stay:

> For pity do not this sad heart belie—
> Even as thou vanishest so shall I die. (I, 259-260)

But Lamia, "growing coy," reminds him that immortals cannot live in the human world "where no joy is,—Empty of immortality and bliss." And when she pretends to say farewell, Lycius, like the "pale warriors" of *La Belle Dame Sans Merci,* turns pale and swoons away. This fit of oblivion, of course, represents the death Lycius prophesied if Lamia should vanish. So far the encounter has pursued the course of *La Belle Dame Sans Merci.*

The difference is that Lamia has been "coy." The "cruel lady" now

> Put her new lips to his, and gave afresh
> The life she had so tangled in her mesh. (I, 294-295)

Lycius thus revived, Lamia "threw the goddess off," and declared herself to be a mortal lady dwelling in Corinth. It might seem that at this point Lycius has died out of process into an immortal bliss. Similarly, the goddess has put off immortality to become a woman. But one recalls the serpentine nature of Lamia and the delicate mockery with which she is described. Moreover, Lycius is not an immortal about to fade into the "green-recessed woods." Instead, he has only swooned; and he will shortly return to Corinth. Similarly, Lamia has put on only the shape and appearance of a woman, but her nature remains untransmuted. She retains her magical powers, and by a spell reduces the distance to Corinth to a few paces.

In other words, the union of Lamia and Lycius is not an actual experience of what is desired. Only in the subjective imagination of Lycius does the situation seem to enact the ideal permanence, just as the love of Hermes and the nymph exists only in the pastoral world, the age-old repository of human wish-fulfillment. When Lycius and Lamia come to Corinth, they take for their dwelling a house where "none but feet divine / Could e'er have touched." Like the "unheard" melodies of the *Ode on a Grecian Urn,* this house represents a withdrawal into purely imaginative activity; for it is known only by Lycius. Other human beings cannot see it, and when subsequently the wedding guests arrive, they

> enter'd marveling: for they knew the street,
> Remember'd it from childhood all complete
> Without a gap, yet ne'er before had seen
> That royal porch, that high-built fair demesne. (II, 152-155)

As a mortal, Lycius must live in Corinth. He cannot escape to the Cretan Elysium where Hermes found his nymph. But he can live in Corinth wholly engaged with his own fantasies and without sharing the life around him, and that is what he does. In short, Lycius is a "dreamer," to borrow the vocabulary of *The Fall of Hyperion,* seeking to become thoughtless or unaware in the fond haven on an unreal paradise, and the poem explores the consequences of such a life. Now as long as the dream is at least partially recognized as only a dream, and in the privacy of the imagination cherished and protected from the intrusion of fact or truth, it can be maintained and enjoyed. As soon as actual human life is vividly represented, it exposes the falsehood of the dream and destroys it. At first, Lycius seems to half-realize that he is indulging a dream. As he enters Corinth with Lamia he endeavors not to be seen—"Muffling his face, of greeting friends in fear." In particular, he fears the sharp eyes of Apollonius. Even to look at Apollonius as he comes near makes Lycius uneasy; for "he seems / The ghost of folly haunting my sweet dreams."

The character of Apollonius, the philosopher, has probably provoked most of the critical disagreement about the poem. A traditional view was that he represents science or "consequitive reasoning" dispelling imagination, and the passage beginning "Do not all charms fly / At the mere touch of cold philosophy?" can be cited:

> Philosophy will clip an Angel's wings,
> Conquer all mysteries by rule and line,
> Empty the haunted air, and gnomed mine—
> Unweave a rainbow, as it erewhile made
> The tender-person'd Lamia melt into a shade. (I, 234-238)

But to interpret the poem in these terms is to make the unwarranted assumption that, if a poem contains a passage of abstract statement, this passage necessarily summarizes the poem. The same notion has vitiated much criticism of the *Ode on a Grecian Urn,* in which the poem has been tortured to make it reveal how or in what sense the urn demonstrates that "Beauty is truth." More recently, critics have pointed out that, however harsh and crabbed Apollonius may be, he is not for that reason the villain of the poem, for Lycius himself is illuded and a dreamer. Both these interpretations are helpful but incomplete. The important point is that within the poem Apollonius is penetrating and Lycius deceived. Lamia is, after all, a serpent, and however loving she may be, she still preys on him, as Apollonius says, by absorbing him to the point that he is incapable of any wider concern. Hers is a frightened, selfish love that would keep its object from growing up in order to continue to possess it. And one might add that from the start Lycius has no chance against this "Virgin . . . in the lore / Of love deep learned to the red heart's core." We know from the letters that Keats was increasingly tending to equate philosophy with truth at the expense of poetry:

> Though a quarrel in the Streets is a thing to be hated, the energies displayed in it are fine . . . This is the very thing in which consists poetry; and if so it is not so fine a thing as philosophy— For the same reason that an eagle is not so fine a thing as a truth.[3]

Again, at the very time he was writing *Lamia,* he said in another letter: "I am convinced more and more every day that (excepting the human friend Philosopher) a fine writer is the most genuine Being in the World." [4] But *Lamia* does not contrast the philosopher with the poet; it contrasts him only with the visionary poet or dreamer.

Apollonius, then, represents a clear though perhaps a single-eyed view of reality. In fact, symbolism of eyes is important in the poem. The vision of Lycius is filled and intoxicated by Lamia:

> his eyes had drunk her beauty up,
> Leaving no drop in the bewildering cup,
> And still the cup was full. (I, 251-253)

Lycius is "blinded" (I, 347), or looks solely into Lamia's "open eyes, / Where he was mirror'd small in paradise" (II, 46-47). "Ah, Goddess, see / Whether my eyes can ever turn from thee," he says (I, 257-258). Her existence increasingly depends on the complete subjective commitment of his eyes to her, which also permits him to see himself mirrored. Only when at the feast he takes his eyes from Lamia to look at Apollonius

[3] *Letters,* ed. Rollins, II, 80-81.
[4] *Letters,* II, 139.

does Lamia begin to vanish; for at this point, as we shall see, only Apollonius, of all the people at the feast, remains fixed in the realities of mortal existence, refusing to enter or share the dream:

> By her glad Lycius sitting, in chief place,
> Scarce saw in all the room another face,
> Till, checking his love trance, a cup he took
> Full brimm'd, and opposite sent forth a look (II, 239-242)

to his old teacher. In contrast to Lycius, Apollonius has "sharp eyes," or "quick eyes" or "eyes severe" (I, 364, 374; II, 157). To the dreamer they are "juggling eyes," or "demon eyes" to be threatened with "blindness," for they banish the dream with their unilluded gaze:

> the sophist's eye,
> Like a sharp spear, went through her utterly,
> Keen, cruel, perceant, stinging. (II, 299-301)

It is true that Apollonius appears as a character of sour disposition. Of course, one could argue that, if he is now harsh to the dreamer, he had previously been a "trusty guide / And good instructor" to Lycius. Moreover, he is seen, to some extent, through the dreamer's eye. But if he is crabbed, that is also partly the attitude of the poem to what he represents. The dreams are sweet, but they are still folly, and however unpleasant, Apollonius's is the completely unilluded perception. To quote from *Hyperion,* he to some extent represents "the pain of truth, to whom 'tis pain." Keats is posing an unhappy dilemma, but it is not the core of the poem. Instead, the poem is largely about the consequences of being a dreamer.

The second part of the poem begins with a "doubtful" conundrum. In keeping with the attitude to reality reflected in the poem, the actual passion of mortals is "love in a hut, with water and a crust." The love of "faery land" is "love in a palace." Neither is satisfactory, but "perhaps at last" the love of faery land is "More grievous torment than a hermit's fast" (II, 1-5). The poem then presents Lamia and Lycius enjoying their bliss. The time is summer and they lie upon a couch, reposing

> Where use had made it sweet, with eyelids closed,
> Saving a tythe which love still open kept,
> That they might see each other while they almost slept.
> (II, 23-25)

This, of course, is the familiar slumberous repose of Keats's mortal-immortal lovers. But Lycius hears the sound of trumpets, which carries his thoughts out of this "purple lined palace" and "into the noisy world almost forsworn." Lamia, "ever watchful,"

> Saw this with pain, so arguing a want
> Of something more, more than her empery
> Of joys. (II, 35-37)

Having recollected the varied life of the human world, Lycius begins to find the dream insufficiently satisfying by itself. Inevitably, he wishes to convert the dream to an actuality in his human life, where Apollonius walks. To translate this into the symbolism of the poem, he and Lamia have been living in "sweet sin," but he now wants to marry her and to have her take a place beside him in his mortal life, together with other companions and interests. As this desire reveals, he has begun to confuse the dream with reality. Up to now, he has not asked Lamia her name, "ever thinking thee," as he says, "Not mortal, but of heavenly progeny, / As still I do." But he now treats her as a mortal woman, browbeating her, and asking whether she has "any mortal name" or any "kinfolk." The questions are similar to the questions addressed to the Grecian urn— "What men or gods are these"—and bespeak the same state of mind; for, as I mentioned, the poet, as the *Ode on a Grecian Urn* begins, has confused "marble men and maidens" with "deities or mortals," and the initial confusion of imaginative vision with earthly reality tends, at the end, to make for a sharper distinction between them. In *Lamia,* however, Keats reaches further. By confusing dream and reality, the dreamer, who is to have an unhappy end, brings them together. Confronted with actuality, the dream is inevitably dispelled. By contrast with the heart's illusion, reality appears meager and crabbed. Meanwhile, the dreamer, having lived so long with his illusion, has become incapable of dwelling in the actual human world. He cannot bear mortal life as it really is, and crumples at the impact.

It is unnecessary to trace the further development of the poem in detail. Lycius decides on a wedding feast to which he will invite his fellow Corinthians. At the feast, things seem at first to go well. With the "wine at flow," the garlands, and the music of powerful instruments—all habitually associated with the paradise that is now viewed as an illusion—the guests seem to enter or share Lycius's state of mind. "Every soul" is "from human trammels freed," and Lamia appears "no more so strange." Only Apollonius remains surely fixed in human realities; but he is enough. When Lycius looks at him, as we have seen, the illusion begins to dissolve under the steady, withering eye of the philosopher. Finally it is destroyed, and Lycius dies.

Of course, Keats's early poetry had often depicted a similar situation. After his first dream-union with Cynthia, Endymion awakens into the life of process and is sore dissatisfied with it:

> all the pleasant hues
> Of heaven and earth had faded: deepest shades
> Were deepest dungeons; heaths and sunny glades
> Were full of pestilent light. (I, 691-694)

Also, shortly after Endymion decides that he has been deluded, has "lov'd a nothing, nothing seen/ Or felt but a great dream" (IV, 637-638), he senses that he is going to die:

> Why, I have been a butterfly, a lord
> Of flowers, garlands, love-knots, silly posies,
> Groves, meadows, melodies, and arbour roses;
> My kingdom's at its death, and just it is
> That I should die with it. (IV, 937-941)

Numerous similar instances might be cited. For example, in the early epistle *To My Brother George,* Keats had written:

> Yet further off, are dimly seen their bowers,
> Of which, no mortal eye can reach the flowers;
> And 'tis right just, for well Apollo knows
> 'Twould make the Poet quarrel with the rose. (lines 43-46)

But if the conclusion of *Lamia* recalls these earlier passages, it does so in a sterner mood. The poet is no longer willing to "quarrel with the rose" for the sake of visionary bowers. We may also recollect that in *The Fall of Hyperion,* where Keats projects himself directly as the protagonist, he almost dies on the steps because he has been a dreamer. In a sense, *Lamia* may be regarded as Keats's version of Wordsworth's

> farewell the heart that lives alone,
> Housed in a dream, at distance from the kind!
> Such happiness, whatever it be known,
> Is to be pitied, for 'tis surely blind.[5]

[5] *Elegiac Stanzas, suggested by a Picture of Peele Castle,* lines 53-56.

The Ode *To Autumn*

by Walter Jackson Bate

Not long after he had first arrived at Winchester, Keats had found a favorite walk that he often took for an hour before dinner. He describes the first part of it in detail to George and Georgiana (September 21), knowing how homesick they were, four thousand miles away, for something that would remind them of England; and the ingenuous phrases of two years before, when he set off to begin *Endymion,* return now in the letters of his last sojourn in the English countryside ("the most beautiful streams about I ever saw"; "the most beautifully clear river"; the "whole Town is beautifully wooded"):

> Now the time is beautiful. I take a walk every day for an hour before dinner and this is generally my walk—I go out at the back gate across one street, into the Cathedral yard, which is always interesting; then I pass under the trees along a paved path, pass the beautiful front of the Cathedral, turn to the left under a stone door way—then I am on the other side of the building—which leaving behind me I pass on through two college-like squares seemingly built for the dwelling place of Deans and Prebendaries —garnished with grass and shaded with trees. Then I pass through one of the old city gates and then you are in one College-Street through which I pass and at the end thereof crossing some meadows and at last a country alley of gardens I arrive, that is, my worship arrives at the foundation of Saint Cross, which is a very interesting old place, both for its gothic tower and alms-square and for the appropriation of its rich rents to a relation of the Bishop of Winchester—Then I pass across St Cross meadows till you come to the most beautifully clear river—now this is only one mile of my walk.

The evenings were becoming cooler, and with them was the suggestion of the coming winter. But the days were still long.

The Sunday after he returned to Winchester from London, he took the same walk out to the St. Cross meadows along the small clear River Itchen (September 19). He mentions the walk in a letter to Reynolds two days later:

> How beautiful the season is now—How fine the air. A temperate sharpness about it . . . I never lik'd stubble fields so much as now—Aye better than the chilly green of the spring. Somehow a stubble plain looks warm—in the same way that some pictures look warm—this struck me so much in my sunday's walk that I composed upon it.

The poem is the last of the great odes, *To Autumn.*

It is because *To Autumn* is so uniquely a distillation, and at many different levels, that each generation has found it one of the most nearly perfect poems in English. We need not be afraid of continuing to use the adjective. In its strict sense the word is peculiarly applicable: the whole is "perfected"—carried through to completion—solely by means of the given parts; and the parts observe decorum (for no other poem of the last two centuries does the classical critical vocabulary prove so satisfying) by contributing directly to the whole, with nothing left dangling or independent. The *Ode to a Nightingale,* for example, is a less "perfect" though a greater poem. The distinctive appeal of *To Autumn* lies not merely in the degree of resolution but in the fact that, in this short space, so many different kinds of resolution are attained.

Most of what Keats had developed in the structure of the ode stanza the previous April and May reappears effortlessly now (the poem seems to have been written very easily). There is only one new variation, simple but altogether appropriate: the ode stanza is given a more prolonged effect; and the prolonging of fulfillment is itself an intrinsic part of the theme of the ode.[1] Not only the formal structure but the whole conception of the odal hymn becomes transparent before its subject. The poet himself is completely absent; there is no "I," no suggestion of the discursive language that we find in the other odes; the poem is entirely concrete, and self-sufficient in and through its concreteness. But if dramatic debate, protest, and qualification are absent, it is not because any premises from which they might proceed are disregarded but because these premises are being anticipated and absorbed at each step. The result (in

[1] The basic ten-line stanza (a Shakespearean quatrain, followed by a Petrarchan sestet: *a b a b c d e c d e*) is now extended to eleven lines. The couplet, which he had wanted to avoid before, is brought back, and placed, not as a tag at the end, but just before the end (first stanza: *a b a b c d e d c c e;* the remaining two: *a b a b c d e c d d e*). The effect of the couplet, placed thus, is to sustain the approaching close at a momentary crest before the stanza subsides in the final line.

contrast to the *Nightingale* or the *Grecian Urn*) is also a successful union of the ideal—of the heart's desire—and reality; of the "greeting of the Spirit" and its object. What the heart really wants is being found (in the first stanza, fullness and completion; in the second, a prolonging of that fulfillment). Here at last is something of a genuine paradise, therefore. It even has its deity—a benevolent deity that wants not only to "load and bless" ("conspiring" with its friend, the sun), but also to "spare," to prolong, to "set budding more." And yet all this is put with concrete exactness and fidelity.

These resolutions are attained partly through still another one to which Keats's poetry has so often aspired: a union of process and stasis (or what Keats had called "stationing"). Each of the three stanzas concentrates on a dominant, even archetypal, aspect of autumn, but, while doing so, admits and absorbs its opposite. The theme of the first is ripeness, of growth now reaching its climax beneath the "maturing sun," as the strain of the weighty fruit bends the apple trees and loads the vines. The cells of the beehives are already brimming over. Yet growth is still surprisingly going on, as autumn and the sun conspire "to set budding more, / And still more, later flowers," and as the bees are deceived into feeling that summer will never end:

> Season of mists and mellow fruitfulness,
>   Close bosom-friend of the maturing sun;
> Conspiring with him how to load and bless
>   With fruit the vines that round the thatch-eves run;
> To bend with apples the moss'd cottage-trees,
>   And fill all fruit with ripeness to the core;
>   To swell the gourd, and plump the hazel shells
>   With a sweet kernel; to set budding more,
> And still more, later flowers for the bees,
> Until they think warm days will never cease,
>   For Summer has o'er-brimm'd their clammy cells.

If, in the first stanza, we find process continuing within a context of stillness and attained fulfillment, in the second—which is something of a reverse or mirror image of the first—we find stillness where we expect process. For now autumn is conceived as a reaper or harvester. Yet it is a harvester that is not harvesting. This benevolent deity is at first motionless, "sitting careless on a granary floor," or asleep on a "half-reap'd furrow," while its "hook / Spares the next swath and all its twinèd flowers" —spares not only the full grain but those new "later flowers" that are interlocking with it. Movement begins only in the latter part of the stanza. Even then it is only suggested in the momentary glimpses of the figure of the gleaner keeping "steady" its "laden head" as it crosses a brook; and autumn then stops again to watch the slow pressing of the apples into cider as the hours pass:

> Who hath not seen thee oft amid thy store?
>   Sometimes whoever seeks abroad may find
> Thee sitting careless on a granary floor,
>   Thy hair soft-lifted by the winnowing wind;
> Or on a half-reap'd furrow sound asleep,
>   Drows'd with the fume of poppies, while thy hook
>   Spares the next swath and all its twinèd flowers:
> And sometimes like a gleaner thou dost keep
>   Steady thy laden head across a brook;
>   Or by a cyder-press, with patient look,
>   Thou watchest the last oozings hours by hours.

There is a hint that the end is approaching—these are the "last oozings" —and the pervading thought in what follows is the withdrawal of autumn, the coming death of the year, and of course the familiar archetypal relevance of the association to our feelings of sequence in our own lives. But if the conception in the previous stanzas has been carried out partly through contrary images—fulfilled growth, while growth still continues; the reaper who is not reaping—the procedure now is almost completely indirect and left solely to inference. The personified figure of autumn is replaced by concrete images of life, and of life unafflicted by any thought of death: the gnats, the hedge crickets, the redbreast. Moreover, it is life that can exist in much the same way at other times than autumn. Only two images are peculiar to the season—the "stubble-plains," and the "full-grown lambs." The mind is free to associate the wailful mourning of the gnats with a funeral dirge for the dying year, but the sound is no more confined to autumn alone than is the "soft-dying" of any day; and if the swallows are "gathering," they are not necessarily gathering for migration:

> Where are the songs of Spring? Ay, where are they?
>   Think not of them, thou hast thy music too,—
> While barrèd clouds bloom the soft-dying day,
>   And touch the stubble-plains with rosy hue;
> Then in a wailful choir the small gnats mourn

Among the river sallows, borne aloft
Or sinking as the light wind lives or dies;
And full-grown lambs loud bleat from hilly bourn;
Hedge-crickets sing; and now with treble soft
The red-breast whistles from a garden-croft;
And gathering swallows twitter in the skies.

The resolutions we have been considering are formal: we have been thinking of the poem as a work of art. To document other considerations that enter would involve (as with every major poem Keats wrote) a recapitulation of much of his life. Yet, since this is the last great lyric that Keats wrote, we may mention three of the many preoccupations and ideals that reach back to the beginning. A principal one is stylistic. We could even start with the first poem he wrote—the *Imitation of Spenser,* with its relative calm. We could then recall the lines in *Sleep and Poetry,* and that early ideal of the dynamic caught momentarily in repose (poetry is "might half slumb'ring on its own right arm"); then the Elgin Marbles, and the various remarks on "intensity" ("Alcibiades, leaning on his Crimson Couch in his Galley, his broad shoulders imperceptibly heaving with the Sea"); and the marginal notes in *Paradise Lost.* This ideal of energy caught in repose pervades the imagery of the poem, and indeed the whole conception and "stationing" of autumn (perhaps the most successful example in English where this "stationing" is obtained with a concept as abstract as a season). A second preoccupation, more nakedly biographical though by no means unconnected with style, is the association of expectance, of waiting, with autumn: we recall that early sonnet, "After dark vapours," in which the almost sick anxiety of waiting for his first volume to appear becomes expressed in images and phrases that anticipate this final ode; and we think of the lines, when *Endymion* was begun in the spring, that leap forward to the thought of concluding it before autumn.

A third consideration, for which there is an equally long history (if the word "long" can be used of so short a life), is his inability to conceive fulfillment without a spring of promise still implicit within it. It may take the form of protest against the starkness of an end, as in those lines Keats wrote in December 1817, after finishing *Endymion* ("In a drear-nighted December"), voicing his envious thought of the bare branches that cannot remember their former green happiness (would that this were so, he goes on, with the human heart); or it may take the form of self-defeating affirmation and desperate hope, as in the *Grecian Urn* (with its "happy, happy boughs" that "cannot shed" their leaves). But the resolution to which he really aspires is that which touched home to him in reading Shakespeare's sonnets two and a half years before:

> When lofty trees I see barren of leaves,
> Which erst from heat did canopy the herd;—

a resolution ("gusto" or "intensity") whereby, as the mind conceives the present, the past and future are simultaneously incorporated in it, and the conception of the "greeting spirit" thus matches, in fidelity to fact, both the unfolding promise and the laden past that are a part of the very nature of the object it is attempting to greet and to rescue into consciousness.

The Two *Hyperions*

by D. G. James

. . . We must now consider the second *Hyperion,* which he had composed in the summer. Once again we have to discuss a fragment, and a shorter fragment than the last. In the first version, Keats had failed to unite idea and narrative. In the second version, he plays boldly and simply *sunders* them. He was aware that in the first version he had not been able to make the narrative bear the load of his meaning; and he now begins by telling us what it is all about and why he wants to tell this narrative. He will explain to us. In the first version, the speech of Oceanus leaves us cloudy and uncertain, and the transformation of Apollo into a god through gazing on the face of Mnemosyne is much too mysterious. He must now in his second version make these things clear—if he can. But how can he explain? How can he make the narrative, as it were, speak to us and explain itself? Even if he is determined to sunder, as I have said, idea and narrative, the exposition of the idea on the one hand, and the narrative on the other, must be formally related to each other. He solves this problem by taking Mnemosyne out of the narrative and by introducing himself into the poem. Mnemosyne will show the story of the warring gods in a vision, and will act as chorus and commentary upon it; Keats will be the audience. But even so, how are Keats and Mnemosyne to come together? There is only one way: in a dream of the poet's mind. Mnemosyne will be a figure in his dream; and the story, shown in vision by Mnemosyne, will be a vision within a dream. This scheme is pretty complicated and does not augur well for the success of the poem.

But at the outset it gives Keats a great advantage. He can now both tell the story (however he may work it out) and explain it. But this advantage is, in another way, a dead loss. For it is Keats's acknowledgment of his failure to make the story self-luminous, to fuse thought and image, the universal and the particular.

It will be recalled that I said three things of the first *Hyperion:* (1) that it was necessary to remove Mnemosyne from the narrative; (2) that Mnemosyne is, in any case, too mysterious and unexplained; (3) that Apollo is a disguise for Keats in particular and poetry in general. In the second version, Keats has tried to do something in respect of all three, which are closely bound up with one another. In the first place, Mnemosyne is taken out of the narrative and is now shown for what she is, a figure out of time. She is now the Eternal Mother of the Muses, to whom Keats can go in this version, as Apollo went in the former. Then, having regard to the third point before speaking of the second, the Apollo of the first version has become the Keats of the second; so that if Mnemosyne has stepped out from the narrative of the gods, so has Apollo, now in the form of Keats. But in this case, were Mnemosyne and Apollo to appear in the story which Mnemosyne will show in vision to Keats? To this question, so far as Apollo is concerned, we cannot give a reply; so far as the second version extends, Apollo is not introduced and we have no means of ascertaining what Keats thought to do. Certainly, this must have presented him with a difficulty, since the poet of the first canto has, it seems, taken on the role of Apollo, as the one who derives "knowledge enormous" from the vision of the face of Mnemosyne. But so far as the question relates to Mnemosyne, we are in a better position to make reply; and the answer reveals with great clearness, I think, one at least of the difficulties which confronted Keats in the making of the second version.

In the first canto the poet finds himself in dream confronted by Mnemosyne (usually in this version, but not always, called Moneta—she is sometimes called Mnemosyne, as in canto 1, l. 331); he is weighed down by the world's pain and speaks to the goddess who uncovers her face. Her face is described in a passage which is famous and which we have already studied. Keats asks to see and understand the "high tragedy" which

> . . . could give so dread a stress
> To her cold lips, and fill with such a light
> Her planetary eyes; and touch her voice
> With such a sorrow?

The reply to this is a vision of Saturn and Thea, as we see them in the beginning of the first version. Mnemosyne explains who they are (ll. 332-5).

Then the poem goes on to further description of Saturn and Thea in their despair. Then, at l. 384, we come to:

> A long awful time
> I look'd upon them: still they were the same;
> The frozen God still bending to the Earth,
> And the sad Goddess weeping at his feet.
> Moneta silent. Without stay or prop
> But my own weak mortality, I bore
> The load of this eternal quietude,
> The unchanging gloom and the three fixed shapes
> Ponderous upon my senses a whole moon.

We have here an uncomfortable feeling that Moneta-Mnemosyne is vaguely a part of the vision as well as a figure outside it who is showing and explaining it to the poet. And in another part (canto 1, l. 226) she describes herself as

> . . . left supreme
> Sole priestess of his [Saturn's] desolation;

So that, even in the second version, she belongs, vaguely, to the narrative of the gods. But she is also an eternal figure, the mother of poets, here conversing with Keats. Now this is clearly a clumsy arrangement, and again, is bound to make Keats's progress in this second version very difficult. And if he was in this difficulty with Mnemosyne, how would the poet who converses with Mnemosyne be connected with Apollo—if Apollo was to appear at all? Thus it is, that if Mnemosyne in the narrative was an embarrassment to Keats, she is also an embarrassment out of it.

To come now to the second of the three points around which this discussion is turning, we see that the second version at least gives Keats the chance of showing us more clearly what he intended by Mnemosyne. The subjective framework of the second version makes possible what the epic and high objective manner of the first rendered very difficult, if not impossible. Released, by his new procedure, from the pressure of the demands of narrative, he can in favourable and leisured circumstances describe at length the face of Mnemosyne, which he did not do in the first version. This passage, in the first version, would have been too remote from action, too rarefied and mystical. Here it is more natural, after the converse Keats and the goddess have had together. Moreover, Keats does not regard the face of Mnemosyne, as he has described it, as satisfying his burning curiosity; and he leads on to the narrative of the wars of the gods by offering the coming story as an explanation of the stress of her lips, the sorrow of her words, and the light of her planetary eyes. The whole story to come will serve the purpose of providing fuller apprehension of the face of Mnemosyne; for it is she, in the second as in the first version, who is central, though in the first she is set in the story and in the second outside it. For in both versions she is the mother of all poets, in her sorrow and suffering and luminous serenity.

Something of the difficulties with which Keats was confronted in the second version will have become clear by this time. He was using now, in order to avoid his former difficulties, a complicated machinery, which must destroy the ease and straightness required of narrative. What we have of the second canto illustrates well enough the awkwardness of his present procedure. It consists of sixty-one lines. The first fifty consist of a speech of Mnemosyne's addressed to the poet, and describing the angry Hyperion in his palace. From this narration, made to the poet of events which he does not see, we pass in ll. 49-56 to a brief description of Keats and Mnemosyne, whereupon Hyperion breaks upon their vision journeying to the Titans in council. Thus has Keats to proceed partly by indirect narration, and partly by direct narration; but also he has from time to time to speak of himself and of Mnemosyne, and of their converse. It seems fairly obvious that the attempt could not continue long.

When we compare the two versions, the outstanding point of contrast is this. The first version is an attempt at high narrative, in a more or less epic manner. Keats was setting out to use his powers of invention. He desired a long, objective poem. In this he fails. He falls back on something less ambitious, reduces his style from anything approaching the epic level, and writes in "cantos" instead of "books"; but above all, he writes something professedly subjective, which is a dream in his own mind, and which is indeed frankly about himself and about poetry. "Invention" has been defeated; and this not only in the first version, but even in the lesser degree required in the second. In adopting the second mode of procedure, Keats obtained, as we have seen, certain advantages; but these advantages also brought complications. In any case, Keats was aware that in the second version he was attempting something intrinsically inferior; for in large measure he had sacrificed objective invention, and his heart could not be in what he was doing in the same degree. This is all the more to be regretted because more than any other member of the Romantic group, Keats saw that what was required was the flowing out of the imagination to apprehend event and circumstance and to show them creatively. He wished to get beyond lyric and subjectivity. He did not wish to talk, but to reveal; not to say, but to show. In *Hyperion,* we may say that the Romantic movement made its greatest effort to create, to go beyond itself into the world. But tragically, like his own Saturn, Keats could not create; Mnemosyne, the mother of the great poets, of whom Keats is one, had failed him. He might, no doubt, have gone on to a finish, as Shelley had done in *Prometheus.* But he chose not to; and his choice was an act of high criticism. The Keats of *Isabella* may, as Arnold said, have lacked criticism. But *Isabella* is no criterion by which to judge Keats. He died in his twenty-seventh year; and his last year was filled with ill health and bitter unhappiness. Yet his mind, in its quality and range, in its passionate desire for what is ideal, in its exquisite and balanced scepticism, in its acceptance, in serenity, of sorrow and suffering, is wonderful to contemplate; and not least wonderful is his failure in what was to be his greatest and most ambitious work. He set himself high standards, in a plenitude of critical power; and he knew what was failure and what was not.

In the course of this long discussion of *Hyperion,* I have left to the end for fuller treatment a crucial consideration to which I have briefly referred at earlier stages. The reader will recall that I suggested that the second Act of *Prometheus,* built around Demogorgon, conflicts with Shelley's use of Greek mythology; and I also suggested that Mnemosyne presents a parallel to Demogorgon in this respect. So far, in speaking of *Hyperion,* I have emphasized the difficulty Keats found in conveying what was in his mind in conceiving her, while also having regard to the demands of narrative, a difficulty which constrained him to resort to another method of procedure in a second version. We must now ask whether this difficulty is not part of a wider one, which in another aspect may consist in placing Mnemosyne, as Keats imagined her, in a setting of Greek mythology.

The reader will have noticed that in what I have said of *Hyperion,* I have interpreted Mnemosyne as symbolizing a perfection and harmony in all existence—an interpretation in accordance with that second strain of speculation and with that second interpretation of "Beauty is Truth" which we have noticed earlier. This interpretation appears, in the light of all we know, to suit the poem most adequately. I need not again comment on the passage in which Keats describes the face of Mnemosyne as it is disclosed to him. It shows a union of extreme suffering with great serenity. As we have seen, on beholding the countenance of the goddess, Keats desires to know what "high tragedy" lies behind, in the "dark secret Chambers" of her mind. If the interpretation by which we have proceeded is correct, Keats, using Mnemosyne as a symbol, sees the world of human experience as a "high tragedy" which is somehow serene and beautiful. Our imagination of Mnemosyne is, I think, best helped by the thought of Cordelia. Indeed it is exceedingly likely that Keats's own imagination was thus helped

> Patience and sorrow strove
> Who should express her goodliest. You have seen
> Sunshine and rain at once; her smiles and tears,
> Were like a better way; those happy smilets
> That play'd on her ripe lip seem'd not to know
> What guests were in her eyes;. which parted thence,
> As pearls from diamonds dropp'd. In brief,
> Sorrow would be a rarity most belov'd,
> If all could so become it.

In lines which follow, Shakespeare appears almost to endow Cordelia with divine attributes:

> . . . there she shook
> The holy water from her heavenly eyes.

Then, after she and Lear have been defeated and captured, these are the words (they are the only words) she speaks:

> We are not the first
> Who, with best meaning, have incurr'd the worst.
> For thee, oppressed King, I am cast down;
> Myself could else out-frown false fortune's frown.

(In passing, we remark that in his first volume of poems Keats had asked, in the opening lines of *Sleep and Poetry,* what can be

> More serene than Cordelia's countenance?)

Now Cordelia, it is true, is set within a tragedy; unlike Mnemosyne, she is a suffering mortal. But it is precisely by the achievement of serenity within the tragic sequence that she rises above it and partakes of what Keats symbolizes in Mnemosyne. Moreover, what Mnemosyne was and symbolized, Keats wished to be, as a poet and as a man. Mnemosyne is indeed a goddess, but in one respect she stands for what Keats hoped the human soul might come to, acceptance of a tragic lot and the attainment of serenity in it, through which what is tragic is also seen as beautiful.

Now I have already said that this "speculation" of Keats is one which the facts of our experience press against with great force. We may, and perhaps ought to, be able to come to the serenity in suffering of which Keats speaks; but we cannot come to the reconciliation with this world of which he speaks. I think it very probable that when Shakespeare was writing *Lear* some such "speculation" as animated Keats animated him also, at least to some extent. But Shakespeare gave his "speculation" no mercy. He did not seek to spare it; and he loaded the play with suffering, both physical and mental, which goes beyond anything in his other plays. And we see, in *Lear,* seeping in unobserved, obscurely determining the choice of phrase and incident, a mode of perception which cannot spring from *this* "speculation," but which arises from another. Lear comes out of the storm into the redeeming love of Cordelia in her superhuman beauty; she receives back the Prodigal, who has fallen from and rejected her, with words that echo the familiar story:

> And wast thou fain, poor father,
> To hovel thee with swine and rogues forlorn,
> In short and musty straw?

Then she is hanged from a beam, and darkness descends on us; but being what we are, it cannot fail to be a darkness of waiting and expectation.

Now when we read the lines of *Hyperion*—

> But for her eyes I should have fled away.
> They held me back, with a benignant light,
> Soft-mitigated by divinest lids
> Half closed, and visionless entire they seem'd
> Of all external things—they saw me not,
> But in blank splendor beam'd like the mild moon,
> Who comforts those she sees not, who knows not
> What eyes are upward cast—

we cannot fail to ask, Who is Mnemosyne,[1] thus suffering and serene, benignant and comforting? If she is benignant she is no mere cosmic tragedy, however harmonious and sublime; and if she gives comfort, she cannot do so as a high impersonal order in which our sorry lives are but contributions to a grand synthesis. We might well curse such a world

[1] She is, of course, for the greater part, called Moneta in the second version.

beyond Good and Evil in place of loving it. But as Keats sees Mnemosyne, as a symbol of the world, there are in her face values of the spirit which no naturalistic scheme can place at the centre of its universe. To be benignant is to be kind and gracious to inferiors; and the benignancy of Mnemosyne is such as is not warranted by Keats's naturalistic speculation, however noble. The awe and worship which Keats extends to her is no mere love of an impersonal order; it is warmed with a love which is saturated by our values. There is then, another "speculation" present in this passage; and it is a "speculation" by no means foreign to Keats and which we have studied in his letters. In *Lear,* Albany says that if

> . . . the heavens do not their visible spirits
> Send quickly down to tame these vile offences,
> It will come,
> Humanity must perforce prey on itself,
> Like monsters of the deep.

No doubt in this Shakespeare was "speculating." And through Keats's apprehension of Mnemosyne there ran, not explicitly perhaps, a "speculation" or perception of the Divine as bearing the woes of the world, and through its labour of vicarious suffering, giving comfort and light to perplexed humanity. We can hardly read the lines which portray the countenance of Mnemosyne without seeing the face of the agonized Christ. Christianity has never said that our hearts can be reconciled to the suffering of the world—it must always remain mysterious to us; it has never said that it may be justified by an "Absolute" to which it is callously condemned to contribute. Instead, Christianity has said that our imaginations can endure the huge reality of evil and pain only when we see it freely endured and borne by God himself. I suggest that something of the sense of this has passed into Keats's lines. At an earlier stage I placed these lines alongside a passage from *The Prelude* in which Wordsworth saw the old soldier as a figure of the utmost religious significance. And when Apollo, in the first version, is shown in his passage into deity after beholding the face of Mnemosyne, Keats can only describe what he undergoes as "dying into life," a phrase in which, better perhaps than in any other, the Christian life is expressed.

It would be as absurd to call Keats a Christian as to use the word for Shelley. He was repelled by Christian dogma as greatly as Shelley. "It is to be lamented," he said of Christ, that his history ". . . was written and revised by Men interested in the pious frauds of Religion." Then he adds that "through all this I see his splendour" (using a word he employs in describing Mnemosyne). Later on, the Romantic movement (if we can allow ourselves to speak thus loosely) will see Christian dogma very differently. But to Shelley and Keats it was anathema. But this did not mean and could not mean that their imaginations were not shot through with ways of feeling and perceiving which could not have been possible to them had they not been reared in a civilization which owed its existence to Christianity. Thus, when they turned to Greek mythology as material through which they could convey what they perceived, it was precisely their unacknowledged Christianity which shattered their antique myths. For if what we have said is true, Mnemosyne is no Greek goddess, and is no more a natural companion for Saturn and Apollo than Demogorgon is for Jove. In the second version she is brought out from this company into that of Keats himself. But this, if in one sense Mnemosyne belongs more to Keats than to Saturn and Apollo, is also a strained situation, so far as Mnemosyne remains at all, if only in name, a Greek goddess. The fact was that it was Greek mythology and not "Miltonic verse" that could only be written "in an artful or rather artist's humour." Keats had an abundance of "artist's humour," as *Lamia* and *The Eve of St. Agnes* in their different ways show. He could *play* the Greek to perfection; but his intentions in *Hyperion* were higher and better than this.

Chronology of Important Dates

1795	Born (October 31), 24 Moorfields Pavement Row, London.
1803	Sent to Clarke school at Enfield.
1804	Keats's father killed in a fall from a horse.
1810	Keats's mother dies (March). His grandmother (Alice Jennings) arranges a trust fund for the Keats children with Richard Abbey and J. N. Sandell as trustees.
1811	Keats removed from school and apprenticed to Thomas Hammond, an apothecary and surgeon, at the village of Edmonton north of London.
1814	Earliest poetry, written at the age of 18 or 19. Keats's grandmother dies in December.
1815	Keats enters Guy's Hospital (October) to study for position as apothecary and surgeon.
1816	First publication (May). Goes to Margate on the coast to write. Returning to London, meets Leigh Hunt and Benjamin Robert Haydon (October), and writes sonnet on *Chapman's Homer* (October). Writes other poems that winter.
1817	First volume appears (March). Keats then goes to Isle of Wight to begin *Endymion,* travels about, visits his friend Benjamin Bailey at Oxford (September), and finishes the poem at the end of November. In December, reviews plays for the *Champion,* writes "Negative Capability" letter, and sees Wordsworth, Lamb, and others at Haydon's "Immortal Dinner."
1818	Reconsideration of his whole career (January-June); begins new Shakespearean sonnets, and writes *Isabella* (March and April); stays in Devon with his ill brother, Tom (March to early May); returns to London; his brother George marries and prepares to emigrate at once to America. June-August: takes walking tour with Charles Brown through northern England and Scotland, and returns ill with a bad cold to find his brother Tom in serious condition. In September and October come the hostile reviews of *Endymion.* Keats begins *Hyperion* (September) and works on it steadily, while nursing Tom, until Tom's death (December 1). Meets Fanny Brawne, September-November. In December, Keats moves into Wentworth Place (Hampstead), renting his rooms from Charles Brown.

1819 *January to early February:* at Chichester and Bedhampton with Charles Brown, and writes *The Eve of St. Agnes.*

February 13-17: Back in Hampstead, writes *The Eve of St. Mark.*

April: Meets Coleridge; the Brawnes move next door; the "Vale of Soul-Making" letter; writes *La Belle Dame Sans Merci* and *Ode to Psyche.*

May: Writes odes—*Nightingale, Grecian Urn, Melancholy,* and *Indolence.*

June to early August: In Isle of Wight, with Charles Brown; writes first half of *Lamia* and part of *The Fall of Hyperion.* The love-letters to Fanny Brawne begin. Writes, with Brown, the play *Otho the Great.*

September: Finishes *Lamia,* and gives up *The Fall of Hyperion,* writes ode *To Autumn,* and returns to London to get work writing for magazines.

October: Becomes ill, and in great desperation. Engagement with Fanny Brawne probably dates from these months. Writes fragment of *King Stephen* and *The Cap and Bells.*

1820 *January:* His brother, George, returns to England briefly to get money from Richard Abbey, guardian and trustee for the Keats children. On February 3, Keats, now gravely ill with tuberculosis, has a hemorrhage in the lungs, and remains confined for months. Moves (May-August) to Kentish Town, when Brown rents his house to others. In July, his third book is published, *Lamia, Isabella, The Eve of St. Agnes, and Other Poems.* On September 18 he sails for Italy, accompanied by Joseph Severn, arriving in Naples on October 31. Traveling to Rome, he finds rooms in 26 Piazza di Spagna (now the Keats-Shelley Memorial House).

1821 Dies on February 23, and is buried in the Protestant Cemetery in Rome.

Notes on the Editor and Authors

WALTER JACKSON BATE, the editor, is Lowell Professor of the Humanities at Harvard. He has written various studies of the period before and during Keats's lifetime, including *From Classic to Romantic, The Achievement of Samuel Johnson,* and some portions of *Criticism: the Major Texts;* and has edited a selection of Burke. Two earlier studies of Keats, *Negative Capability* and *The Stylistic Development of Keats,* have been followed by his recent critical biography, *John Keats.* He is currently writing on Coleridge, and editing three volumes for the Yale Edition of Johnson.

HAROLD BLOOM, Associate Professor of English at Yale, is the author of *Blake's Apocalypse: a Study in Poetic Argument, Shelley's Mythmaking,* and *The Visionary Company: a Reading of English Romantic Poetry.*

DOUGLAS BUSH, Gurney Professor of English at Harvard, has written copiously on literature from the Greeks to the present day. His works include *Classical Influences in English Literature, Mythology and the Renaissance Tradition, Mythology and the Romantic Tradition, The Renaissance and English Humanism, English Literature in the Earlier Seventeenth Century* (Vol. V in the *Oxford History*), *Science and English Poetry, Paradise Lost in Our Time,* and *English Poetry . . . Chaucer to the Present;* editions of Shakespeare, Milton, and Keats; and many articles on Keats and other writers. He has just finished a short biography of Milton, and is completing one on Keats in the same series.

T. S. ELIOT, one of the foremost poets and critics of our century, delivered his Charles Eliot Norton lectures on poetry at Harvard in 1932-33.

RICHARD HARTER FOGLE, Chairman of the English Department at Tulane University, is the author of *The Imagery of Keats and Shelley, The Idea of Coleridge's Criticism, Hawthorne's Fiction,* and *Melville's Shorter Tales.*

DAVID GWILYM JAMES, Vice-Chancellor of the University of Southampton, is the author of *Scepticism and Poetry, The Romantic Comedy, The Life of Reason, The Dream of Learning,* and *Matthew Arnold and the Decline of English Romanticism.*

DAVID PERKINS, Professor of English at Harvard, and author of several articles on subjects ranging from the Elizabethans to T. S. Eliot, has written two books on the romantics—*The Quest for Permanence: the Symbolism of Wordsworth, Shelley, and Keats,* and *Wordsworth and the Poetry of Sincerity*—and is currently completing a critical anthology of romantic literature.

JACK STILLINGER, Associate Professor of English at the University of Illinois, has written several articles on Keats, has edited Wordsworth, and is now completing an edition of the *Letters of Charles Brown* and a book on romantic poetry. He assisted Hyder Rollins in completing the standard edition of Keats's *Letters.*

EARL WASSERMAN, Chairman of the English Department at The Johns Hopkins University, and editor of *Modern Language Notes* and the *Journal of English Literary History,* is the author of *The Finer Tone: Keats' Major Poems, Elizabethan Poetry in the Eighteenth Century, The Scholarly Origin of the Elizabethan Revival, Pope's Epistle to Bathurst, The Subtler Language: Critical Readings of Neoclassic and Romantic Poems,* and many articles on eighteenth century and romantic literature.

Selected Bibliography

I. *Editions*

Of the following works, arranged chronologically, the standard text for the poetry is that of H. W. Garrod, and for the letters that of H. E. Rollins. Garrod's edition, however, gives no explanatory notes, and is therefore of little help to the general student. Of editions of the complete poems, that with the most helpful annotation is still the edition of Ernest de Selincourt (5th ed., 1926). For selections (of both poetry and letters) the best is that of Douglas Bush (1959).

Poems of John Keats, ed. Ernest de Selincourt (5th ed., London, 1926).

Poetical Works, ed. H. W. Garrod (Oxford, 1939; rev. ed. 1958).

Letters of John Keats, ed. Hyder E. Rollins, 2 vols. (Cambridge, Mass., 1958).

Selected Poems and Letters, ed. Douglas Bush (Boston, 1959).

II. *Biography*

The five major biographies are listed below, in order of appearance, together with a principal source book (*The Keats Circle*). The biographies of Colvin, Lowell, and Bate are in the "life and works" tradition, while those of Miss Hewlett and Miss Ward are concerned more particularly with the life of Keats. Of these five biographies, two (Colvin and Lowell) are a little outdated as far as biographical fact is concerned; but in each case the critical discussion is still valuable and both books remain important as pioneer works. Miss Hewlett's biography incorporates new detail while also presenting the contemporaneous setting of the Keats family. The recent biographies by Miss Ward and W. J. Bate incorporate further details—Miss Ward concentrating on the life and personal character of Keats, as a human being, and Bate on the writings and Keats's relation to tradition.

Colvin, Sir Sidney, *John Keats: His Life and Poetry, His Friends, Critics, and After-Fame* (New York, 1920).

Lowell, Amy, *John Keats,* 2 vols. (Boston and New York, 1925).

Rollins, Hyder E. (ed.), *The Keats Circle,* 2 vols. (Cambridge, Massachusetts, 1948).

Hewlett, Dorothy, *A Life of John Keats* (2nd. ed. rev., New York, 1950).

Ward, Aileen, *John Keats: the Making of a Poet* (New York, 1963).

Bate, W. J., *John Keats* (Cambridge, Massachusetts, 1963).

III. *Selected Critical Studies*

For a detailed list of critical studies, readers may consult J. R. MacGillivray, *Keats: A Bibliography and Reference Guide* (Toronto, 1949), and the annual bibliography in the Keats-Shelley Journal that began with its second issue (1953).

Bate, W. J., *The Stylistic Development of Keats* (New York, 1945). Concerned principally with versification. Cf. "Keats's Style," *The Major English Romantic Poets,* ed. Thorpe, Baker, and Weaver (Carbondale, Ill., 1957).

Beyer, Werner, *Keats and the Daemon King* (New York, 1947). Concerned with literary sources.

Bloom, Harold, *The Visionary Company* (New York, 1961). Succinct, suggestive explications of the major poems of the principal romantic poets.

Bush, Douglas, *Mythology and the Romantic Tradition* (Cambridge, Mass., 1937); (New York, 1957). "Keats and His Ideas," *Major English Romantic Poets,* ed. Thorpe, Baker, and Weaver (Carbondale, Ill., 1957).

Caldwell, James R., *John Keats' Fancy: the Effect on Keats of the Psychology of His Day* (Ithaca, 1945).

Finney, Claude L., *The Evolution of Keats's Poetry,* 2 vols. (Cambridge, Mass., 1936). Richly detailed, especially about Keats's sources.

Fogle, Richard H., *The Imagery of Keats and Shelley* (Chapel Hill, N.C., 1949).

Gittings, Robert, *John Keats: The Living Year* (Cambridge Mass., 1954). Concerned with literary sources and biographical incident relevant to Keats's poetry from September, 1818, to September, 1819.

James, D. G., *The Romantic Comedy* (London, 1948).

Leavis, F. R., *Revaluation* (London, 1936).

Muir, Kenneth (ed.), *John Keats: A Reassessment* (Liverpool, 1958).

Murry, J. M., *Keats and Shakespeare* (London, 1930); and *Keats* (New York, 1955), the latter being a revision and enlargement of two other works on Keats, *Studies in Keats* (London, 1930; rev. 1939) and *The Mystery of Keats* (London, 1949).

Perkins, David, *The Quest for Permanence: The Symbolism of Wordsworth, Shelley, and Keats* (Cambridge, Mass., 1959); and "Keats's Odes and Letters: Recurrent Diction and Imagery," *Keats-Shelley Journal,* II (1953), 51-60.

Ridley, M. R., *Keats' Craftsmanship* (Oxford, 1933). Keats's development interpreted through a study of his manuscript revisions.

Sherwood, Margaret, "Keats' Imaginative Approach to Myth," *Undercurrents of Influence in English Romantic Poetry* (Cambridge, Mass., 1934).

Slote, Bernice, *Keats and the Dramatic Principle* (Lincoln, Neb., 1958).

Stillinger, Jack, "The Hoodwinking of Madeline: Skepticism in *The Eve of St. Agnes,*" *Studies in Philology,* LVIII (1961), 533-555.

Thorpe, Clarence D., *The Mind of John Keats* (New York, 1926). A pioneer work in the study of Keats's thought.

Wasserman, Earl R., *The Finer Tone: Keats' Major Poems* (Baltimore, 1953). A perceptive and detailed explication of the odes, *La Belle Dame Sans Merci, The Eve of St. Agnes,* and *Lamia.*

TWENTIETH CENTURY VIEWS

British Authors

Jane Austen, edited by Ian Watt (S-TC-26)
The Beowulf Poet, edited by Donald K. Fry (S-TC-82)
Blake, edited by Northrop Frye (S-TC-58)
Byron, edited by Paul West (S-TC-31)
Coleridge, edited by Kathleen Coburn (S-TC-70)
Conrad, edited by Marvin Mudrick S-TC-53)
Dickens, edited by Martin Price (S-TC-72)
John Donne, edited by Helen Gardner (S-TC-19)
Dryden, edited by Bernard N. Schilling (S-TC-32)
T. S. Eliot, edited by Hugh Kenner (S-TC-2)
Fielding, edited by Ronald Paulson (S-TC-9)
Forster, edited by Malcolm Bradbury (S-TC-59)
Hardy, edited by Albert Guérard (S-TC-25)
Hopkins, edited by Geoffrey H. Hartman (S-TC-57)
A. E. Housman, edited by Christopher Ricks (S-TC-83)
Samuel Johnson, edited by Donald J. Greene (S-TC-48)
Ben Jonson, edited by Jonas A. Barish (S-TC-22)
Keats, edited by Walter Jackson Bate (S-TC-43)
D. H. Lawrence, edited by Mark Spilka (S-TC-24)
Marlowe, edited by Clifford Leech (S-TC-44)
Andrew Marvell, edited by George deF. Lord (S-TC-81)
Milton, edited by Louis L. Martz (S-TC-60)
Modern British Dramatists, edited by John Russell Brown (S-TC-74)
Oscar Wilde, edited by Richard Ellmann (S-TC-87)
Restoration Dramatists, edited by Earl Miner (S-TC-64)
Samuel Richardson, edited by John Carroll (S-TC-85)
Shakespeare: The Comedies, edited by Kenneth Muir (S-TC-47)
Shakespeare: The Histories, edited by Eugene M. Waith (S-TC-45)
Shakespeare: The Tragedies, edited by Alfred Harbage (S-TC-40)
G. B. Shaw, edited by R. J. Kaufmann (S-TC-50)
Shelley, edited by George M. Ridenour (S-TC-49)
Spenser, edited by Harry Berger, Jr. (S-TC-80)
Laurence Sterne, edited by John Traugott (S-TC-77)
Swift, edited by Ernest Tuveson (S-TC-35)
Thackeray, edited by Alexander Welsh (S-TC-75)
Dylan Thomas, edited by Charles B. Cox (S-TC-56)
Yeats, edited by John Unterecker (S-TC-23)

TWENTIETH CENTURY VIEWS

European Authors

BAUDELAIRE, edited by Henri Peyre (S-TC-18)
SAMUEL BECKETT, edited by Martin Esslin (S-TC-51)
BRECHT, edited by Peter Demetz (S-TC-11)
CAMUS, edited by Germaine Brée (S-TC-1)
CHEKHOV, edited by Robert Louis Jackson (S-TC-71)
DANTE, edited by John Freccero (S-TC-46)
DOSTOEVSKY, edited by René Wellek (S-TC-16)
EURIPIDES, edited by Erich Segal (S-TC-76)
FLAUBERT, edited by Raymond Giraud (S-TC-42)
GOETHE, edited by Victor Lange (S-TC-73)
HOMER, edited by George Steiner and Robert Fagles (S-TC-15)
IBSEN, edited by Rolf Fjelde (S-TC-52)
KAFKA, edited by Ronald Gray (S-TC-17)
LORCA, edited by Manuel Duran (S-TC-14)
MALRAUX, edited by R. W. B. Lewis (S-TC-37)
THOMAS MANN, edited by Henry Hatfield (S-TC-36)
MOLIÈRE, edited by Jacques Guicharnaud (S-TC-41)
PIRANDELLO, edited by Glauco Cambon (S-TC-67)
PROUST, edited by René Girard (S-TC-4)
SARTRE, edited by Edith Kern (S-TC-21)
SOPHOCLES, edited by Thomas Woodard (S-TC-54)
STENDHAL, edited by Victor Brombert (S-TC-7)
TOLSTOY, edited by Ralph E. Matlaw (S-TC-68)
VIRGIL, edited by Steele Commager (S-TC-62)
VOLTAIRE, edited by William F. Bottiglia (S-TC-78)

TWENTIETH CENTURY VIEWS

American Authors

AUDEN, edited by Monroe K. Spears (S-TC-38)
STEPHEN CRANE, edited by Maurice Bassan (S-TC-66)
EMILY DICKINSON, edited by Richard B. Sewall (S-TC-28)
EMERSON, edited by Milton R. Konvitz
and Stephen E. Whicher (S-TC-12)
FAULKNER, edited by Robert Penn Warren (S-TC-65)
F. SCOTT FITZGERALD, edited by Arthur Mizener (S-TC-27)
ROBERT FROST, edited by James M. Cox (S-TC-3)
HAWTHORNE, edited by A. N. Kaul (S-TC-55)
HEMINGWAY, edited by Robert P. Weeks (S-TC-8)
HENRY JAMES, edited by Leon Edel (S-TC-34)
SINCLAIR LEWIS, edited by Mark Schorer (S-TC-6)
ROBERT LOWELL, edited by Thomas Parkinson (S-TC-79)
MELVILLE, edited by Richard Chase (S-TC-13)
ARTHUR MILLER, edited by Robert W. Corrigan (S-TC-84)
MODERN AMERICAN DRAMATISTS, edited by Alvin B. Kernan (S-TC-69)
O'NEILL, edited by John Gassner (S-TC-39)
POE, edited by Robert Regan (S-TC-63)
EZRA POUND, edited by Walter Sutton (S-TC-29)
WALLACE STEVENS, edited by Marie Borroff (S-TC-33)
THOREAU, edited by Sherman Paul (S-TC-10)
MARK TWAIN, edited by Henry Nash Smith (S-TC-30)
EDITH WHARTON, edited by Irving Howe (S-TC-20)
WHITMAN, edited by Roy Harvey Pearce (S-TC-5)
W. C. WILLIAMS, edited by J. Hillis Miller (S-TC-61)